THE MODERN NATIONS IN
HISTORICAL PERSPECTIVE

ROBIN W. WINKS, *General Editor*

The volumes in this series deal with individual nations or groups of closely related nations throughout the world, summarizing the chief historical trends and influences that have contributed to each nation's present-day character, problems, and behavior. Recent data are incorporated with established historical background to achieve a fresh synthesis and original interpretation.

JOHN F. CADY, the author of this volume in the Modern Nations in Historical Perspective series, is Distinguished Professor of History at Ohio University. He has extensive firsthand knowledge of Southeast Asia, having taught in Burma before World War II, then serving as Burma Analyst for the Office of Strategic Services from 1943-45 and as State Department officer for South and Southeast Asia from 1945-49, and having studied in Burma as a Fulbright Scholar and Guggenheim Fellow. He is also the author of *Southeast Asia: Its Historical Development*; *A History of Modern Burma*; and *The Roots of French Imperialism in Eastern Asia*, which was awarded the Carnegie Endowment Prize of the American Historical Association.

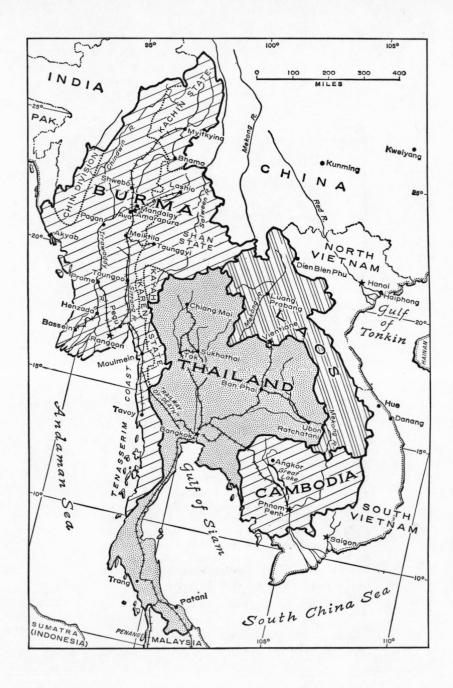

THAILAND, BURMA, LAOS, & CAMBODIA

JOHN F. CADY

A SPECTRUM BOOK

Prentice-Hall, Inc.

Englewood Cliffs, New Jersey

Current printing (last number):

10 9 8 7 6 5 4 3 2 1

The selection of the four Theravada Buddhist countries of Southeast Asia, Burma, Thailand, Cambodia, and Laos, as the subject of a single monograph is based on the assumption that their historical and cultural development, deriving in part from common Indian associations, can be correlated in a meaningful way. The more or less arbitrary exclusion of Vietnam from consideration in this connection, despite the substantial presence of Mahayana Buddhism in the area, can be justified on the grounds that its civilization and governmental forms were adapted mainly from the Chinese tradition rather than from the Indian. The temporary political association of Cambodia and Laos with Annam and Cochin-China for a little more than a half a century within the perimeter of French Indochina did not serve to bridge over in any substantial fashion the basic cultural and historic divergencies. French rule changed very little the traditional patterns of society, government, and religion of the subject peoples of the Mekong Valley.

This is not to suggest that the four Theravada Buddhist countries are in any sense carbon copies of each other. The Thai and Lao peoples of the Mekong Valley come closest to being identical for they are ethnically akin; Lao culture can be characterized as a provincial variant of Siamese civilization. But mountainous areas of Laos contain a number of tribal peoples, the non-Buddhist Thai tribes, the half Chinese Meo and Mau and the primitive Kha. The latter groups are not to be found within the largely homogenized peoples of Siam, who have also been subjected to a degree of cultural sophistication not to be found in the trans-Mekong area. In the larger regional context, the long history of the Mons, Pyu, Burmans, and Shans of Burma proper and the Malays, Mons, Khmers, and Thai in the eastern area, has contributed not only significant linguistic and cultural variations but also the development of long-sustained political rivalries. Divergencies have been further extended in modern times by Siam's avoidance of colonial status while Burma was being incorporated into British India and Laos and Cambodia were becoming French protectorates. The most fruitful areas for direct comparison and contrast are modern Burma and Siam, but the relationships of all Indochinese people are conditioned by their historic experiences.

173648

A brief explanation is in order regarding the use of terms. The two adjectival forms, Burman and Burmese, will be used to refer respectively to the ethnic majority group via the former term, and to the more general characteristics relating to Burma as a whole via the latter, including minority peoples. Siam was the proper political designation of the nation state prior to the formal adoption of the term Thailand in 1939. The ethnic majority group has always been called Thai, whereas the term Siamese refers to aspects characterizing the country of Siam. The Shans of Burma are ethnically very much the same as the Thai, but they have experienced little or no political connection with Siam. Cambodia is the modern name for the much larger medieval Khmer state, which dominated much of Indochina from the late 600's to the final subordination of Angkor to Siam around 1430. The terms Indochina and Indochinese will refer to the peninsula as a whole, excepting the lower Malay peninsula.

Because the occupants of wet-rice cultivated areas were alone capable of developing extensive social, economic, and political systems, the main currents of history have bypassed the ethnically diverse and often non-Buddhist hillside cultivators who occupy the watershed areas. The hillside peoples everywhere maintain with great tenacity their traditional patterns of social organization and livelihood. These minority groups are quite properly the subject of anthropological examination, but because they influenced the main stream of historical development only in spasmodic fashion, they will be considered only when circumstances demand.

J.F.C.

Contents

ONE

CURRENT REALITIES AND

INTERRELATIONSHIPS

Spirit Worship, Hinduism, and Indian Patterns of Kingship

The major peoples of Buddhist Southeast Asia share today a similar cultural heritage. Common social aspects indigenous to these peoples include: the wide prevalence of matrilineal kinship groups and the consequent patterns of village autonomy based on such kinship ties, the governing of society by hereditary headmen and elders, and the social control of water and land resources. Another significant aspect of this common cultural heritage is that of spirit worship.

The world of the Southeast Asian villager was, and still is, dominated by the belief in the existence of a great variety of spirits, sometimes benevolent but more often vindictive and capricious. Many such spirits were associated with topographical phenomena, such as lakes, rivers, mountains, isolated trees, and particular sections of the jungle. Placation of these spirits played a prominent role in agriculture, and was equally important in the maintenance of health and general good fortune. Villagers paid tribute annually to special pantheons, customarily made up of the spirits of victims of violence or tragedy, such as childbirth, murder, or accident. Guardian spirits, derived from victims sacrificed at the spot, were utilized on occasion for purposes of protecting gateways and the walls of fortresses. Friendly spirits were sometimes enlisted to aid military enterprises in fighting against spirits of the enemy. Consequently, much of the time of the villager, and of the royal courts as well, was taken up by efforts to enlist the aid and to satisfy the demands of the spirit world.

Another common cultural bond in Buddhist Southeast Asia is the impact which Indian culture had on the area. The cultural affinity which developed during the first millennium A.D. between the peoples of peninsular Indochina and those of India owed much to the retention and refinement by Hinduism of animistic beliefs and practices which were originally similar to those of the Southeast Asians. Śiva and Vishnu cults in particular, while in the process of development, integrated many ancient animistic cults and articulated them within the intellectual framework of Sanskrit literature. The Devangari writing system used in Sanskrit literature and the Pali language in which the Theravada Buddhist scriptures were recorded supplied for centuries the principal media for written communication and the patterns for interpretative thought and expression throughout most of Indochina.

The elevation of a new ruler to the status of divine kingship in the Indian pattern was accomplished through the magical ministrations of the court Brahmans. The traditional coronation ceremonies, which authenticated the ruler as the divine *avator* of Vishnu, Indra, or Śiva, involved the fashioning of impressive royal genealogies, the granting of the symbols of royal regalia such as the sacred sword and the white umbrella, and the lustral water bath. At the accession of new rulers, the Brahmans also supervised the drinking of impregnated oath water by all high officials. These traditional ceremonies survived to modern times, so that princely status, however discredited and tawdry it may have come to be, continued to convey an aura of qualitative distinction and inherent authenticity. Thus the coronation ceremonies of Burma's last king, Thibaw, held in 1878, like those of more recent rulers crowned at Bangkok, Luang Prabang, and Phnom Penh, followed a pattern based on the traditional Indian practice of exalting the kingly office to divine status.

Needless to say, this long-established Indian kingship tradition militates effectively today against popular acceptance of Western principles of popular sovereignty and representative government. All of the four countries under discussion are currently (1966) governed by authoritarian regimes. Military control is nakedly applied in the case of Burma, where the princely tradition has been broken, but the peasants still look for a divine king. Thailand's army rulers have operated as a rule behind the thin façade of constitutional forms which date from 1932, but these constitutional forms have been honored only in perfunctory fashion. A more meaningful basis of Thai governmental authority is that derived from the surviving symbolism of kingship and the royal palace. The three main factions which developed in postwar French Laos, furthermore, have all been headed by authentic princes, including even the pro-Communist Pathet Lao leader, Prince Souphanouvong. Ex-King and Premier Norodom Sihanouk of Cambodia also possesses, by virtue of his royal lineage, intrinsic authority in his own right, a factor which as an astute politician he has skilfully exploited.

The Common Bond of Theravada Buddhism

The Buddhist religion, which also entered Southeast Asia from India in the early centuries A.D., developed a popularity and social significance which Hinduism could not match. Buddhism rejected caste, the elaborate pantheon of the Hindu gods, and the priestly functions of the Brahmans. It offered instead the model of the Buddhist saint who was both a recluse and a sage. Buddhism also affirmed for every man the possibility of escape from the endless and burdensome gyrations of life's wheel of existence through the conquest of desire and the following of the eightfold path of righteous living. The broadly humanitarian character of Buddhism increased its popularity as a faith. Of the two variant forms of Buddhism, which will be described in Chapter Two, only the earlier Theravada tradition (of the teachers) survived in Indianized Southeast Asia.

In all Buddhist countries the proudest boast of every ruler related to his patronage of the three jewels of Buddha, the Sangha (monkhood), and the dharma (law or discipline). Under governmental guidance in medieval times the earlier unorganized routines of wandering mendicants were slowly superseded by the Sangha, or Buddhist monastic hierarchy. As patrons of the order, the rulers designated a Sangharajah (Thathanabaing in Burma) as a kind of ruling primate. He was held responsible for supervising the internal discipline of the order but was denied any formal political or governmental role. The royal Buddhist council, which was presided over by the Sangharajah and included the heads of various minor sects, acted as final arbiter in matters of doctrine and discipline. Regional "bishops," district abbots, and their various assistants completed the structure of the hierarchy. Lay royal officials adjudicated unresolved disputes within the Sangha, enforced disciplinary decisions where necessary, and supervised the land titles of the monasteries. The monkhood profited richly from royal patronage, but accepted in turn a substantial measure of royal control. The monks were revered by the people but were theoretically isolated from politics, save when the ruler might request their services as peacemakers or as envoys in important diplomatic negotiations.

Indian Buddhism in the Theravada form has survived only in Ceylon and in continental Southeast Asia. The authenticity of Theravada standards of ordination and discipline have been renewed from time to time by the sending of religious missions to older Sinhalese Buddhist centers such as Kandy. On one occasion following the South Indian invasion of Ceylon in the eleventh century, the renewal of standards was drawn from Mon Burma.

Despite the very substantial measure of homogeneity prevailing within Burmese, Thai, and Cambodian society and religion, the three have never been completely identical because each made local accommodations to indigenous patterns of spirit worship. Although the canonical traditions of the *Pali* scriptures still provided the ideal basis for Buddhism, the actual religious practices of particular Buddhist adherents reflected cult traditions unrelated to the canon. These included annual ceremonies connected with fertility rites, planting and harvest routines, plus life-cycle celebrations, divination, and practices associated with the prevention of misfortune and disease.

The resulting religious amalgam in each case was something more than a syncretic accumulation of variant elements, for the greater Buddhist tradition and the lesser spirit world cults were inextricably mingled. Symbolisms of both systems were widely shared. Many Buddhists still regard the techniques of numerology, astrology, and shamanistic dealing with the spirit world as practically useful for satisfying mundane needs (health, good fortune, prosperity), even though all of life's vicissitudes could be rationalized by reference to Buddhist Karma. The principles of the Theravada faith, including Buddhist ideas of merit and karma, provided a uniform framework for the totality of life views, a kind of highest common denominator for ecumenical relationships in the great Pali tradition.

Historical Relationships and Rivalries

In addition to contributing lasting patterns in areas of government and religion, the history of the Buddhist peoples of Southeast Asia also provided a tradition of rivalries and antipathies which color the present-day outlook. For example, Cambodian hostility to Vietnamese expansion dates from early times, and came to a head during the fifteenth century following the Vietnamese conquest and occupation of the buffer state of Champa. In the same century, the newly established Thai state of Ayuthia (founded 1350) completely destroyed the Cambodian capital of Angkor in 1432. Thus Cambodia's problem of defending itself against its traditionally hostile neighbors, Vietnam and Siam, today assumes far greater importance at Phnom Penh than the possibly ephemeral and seemingly more remote considerations connected with the cold war between Americans and the Chinese Communists.

The Buddhist Lao peoples inhabiting the middle Mekong River valley and its tributaries are closely akin to the Siamese ethnically, linguistically, and culturally. Furthermore, the state of Laos within its present boundaries possesses little or no nationalist tradition. The southern Laotian principality of Champassak was vassal to Siam for more than four centuries prior to the French arrival in 1893. The central region around Vientiane was from time to time a center of resistance to Siam's overlordship and was not completely incorporated as an integral part of the Siamese kingdom until 1826. The northerly Lao kingdom of Luang Prabang has traditionally enjoyed a substantial measure of autonomy, but it preferred vassalage to the kindred Thai rather than to the periodic Burmese or Vietnamese invaders. The trans-Mekong Lao accepted French protection in the late nineteenth century without protest partly in order to escape Bangkok's control, which was strongly asserted after 1826. The animist Black Thai in the north and the various hillside cultivators of the Annamite cordillera, Kha, Meo, Man, and Moi, harbored little affection for the politically and culturally dominant Buddhist Lao of the Mekong Valley. In Laos, as in Cambodia, present-day events cannot be understood apart from such historical antecedents.

Siam's national tradition centers around its role as leader of the Thai peoples, who overflow its boundaries into Burma's Shan states and into Laos beyond the Mekong. Burma's coastal region of Tenasserim has been historically as often Siamese as Burmese politically, while most of the Malay sultanates down to 1874 acknowledged nominal vassalage to Bangkok. Thai irredentist ambitions found expression in World War II, when Bangkok managed with Japanese help to recover temporarily several border areas ceded to French Indochina after 1893, plus frontier states in British Malaya and in Burma's Shan states. The enforced surrender of these territories after the war did not mean that Thailand was reconciled to her restricted borders, particularly those with Laos and Cambodia. Rightist elements in the Laotian feud, particularly in Champassak, found sympathy and support in Thailand, while Thai relations with the hypersensitive Cambodian authorities on both territorial and ideological grounds continued to be acrimonious. A dispute over the Cambodian borderline temple of Preah Vihear was settled in 1962 only by special adjudication of the World Court.

Siam's traditional relations with the kingdom of Burma since the sixteenth century have been perennially hostile. Burmese armies of the Toungoo dynasty during the latter half of the 1500s staged repeated raids on Siam and its Lao vassals, and the border principality of Chiengmai was ruled from Burma for a number of decades. The Burmese attacks were revived by the Konbaung dynasty in the middle eighteenth century, culminating in the wanton destruction of Ayuthia in 1767, an act which the Thai have never forgotten. Happily, as a result of labored efforts on both sides since the end of World War II, this traditional rivalry is currently held in abeyance, although Burmese have accused the Thai of negligence in controlling the activities of Karen dissidents and Kuomintang refugees along the border. A helpful border agreement was signed in May 1963.

The meager commercial relations existing between the Buddhist lands of Southeast Asia have contributed little to soften the harsh impact of historic antipathies. The exceptions are landlocked Laos, which has found a useful commercial outlet only via Thailand, and Burma's Shan states, whose trading connections are via the upper Sittang and Irrawaddy valleys of Burma proper. Cambodia's trade during the French period found its principal outlet through the port of Saigon. Even if the topographical watersheds inhabited by hill-cultivating tribesmen did not act as trade barriers, the basic products of Burma, Siam, and Cambodia, rice, timber, and minerals, are so nearly identical that they have provided little incentive for trade. Therefore, we should note that the striking similarities of religion, social organization, and governmental institutions which characterize the Theravada Buddhist states find no counterpart in traditions of commercial or political cooperation.

Postwar Burma

Burma's outlook since achieving its freedom in 1948 has been dominated by its concern with establishing genuine economic and political independence. Behind this concern is Burma's determination to avoid again becoming a tragic battlefield for world giants, as was the country's fate in World War II. Because of local Communist involvement in the rebellions which engulfed the new state in 1948-49, coupled with the acceptance of British Commonwealth assistance against the rebels, Burma's initial international orientation was generally pro-Attlee, pro-Nehru, and pro-Western. This did not, however, prevent Burma from being the first non-Communist state to accord recognition to Red China in early 1950. The general ineffectiveness and inadequacy of subsequent American economic assistance plus the failure of Washington to accept responsibility for halting the arming from Formosa of Chinese Nationalist refugees along Burma's China border caused Rangoon authorities to cancel American aid abruptly in 1953. It was revived only briefly from 1959 to 1962.

A deliberate policy of nonalignment in the cold war has been pursued by Burma fairly consistently since 1953. This policy was coupled with a willingness to accept aid from any quarter if given without strings, and an alleged determination to judge particular international issues on their respective merits. Relations between Premier Nu's government and that of India's Nehru were very cordial, and those with London were only slightly less so. Chairman Khrushchev's generous offer made to Burma in 1956 to contribute a hospital, a technical institute, and a sports stadium was accepted by Burma. It was accompanied at the time by barter trade agreements with various Communist states, including China, which were designed to relieve Burma's rice glut. Eventually United States aid for road construction was again solicited on a modest basis. But the crucial aspect of the country's external relations concerned neighboring China. Burma wanted to settle the border dispute and also to end Chinese support of Communist subversionary activities within Burma itself.

Peking's initial response to Burma's early recognition of the Chinese Communist regime in 1950 was decidedly cool. When the long-delayed exchange of ambassadors was finally made in mid-1951, Red China appeared to be more interested in obtaining the allegiance of the several hundred thousand Chinese residents within Burma rather than in lending support to the discredited Communist rebellion, which in any case had been initiated in 1948 under the aegis of Moscow. Much to Burma's relief, China subsequently elected not to regard the Kuomintang refugee problem along the Burma border as an item of dispute with Rangoon. Meanwhile, the general indecisiveness of the United Nations police action in South Korea disillusioned earlier Burmese expectations that genuine protection against potential Chinese aggression could be provided by the world organization. The alternative course was to cultivate friendly political and commercial relations with an increasingly powerful China and to negotiate persistently for a boundary agreement with Peking. These objectives were steadfastly pursued by successive Rangoon governments, despite prevailing differences regarding anti-Communist policies domestically and political divergencies along personal lines.

The Sino-Burman boundary settlement was finally consummated in 1960-61 by General Ne Win and by Premier Nu in a fashion regarded as highly satisfactory from the Burmese point of view, even though it involved two significant concessions in China's favor. Burma pledged itself not to permit its territory to become a base for political or military operations hostile to China and also agreed to continue efforts to develop economic and cultural intercourse. The effects of this agreement, containing as it did an implied if slight limitation of Burma's sovereign independence, virtually ended the prospect for Burma's participation in any kind of Southeast Asian security pact, a result which may have been China's principal objective. Burmese authorities later in 1962 apparently condoned China's attacks on India, which constituted, among other things, a kind of blackmail procedure on China's part to force smaller Asian states into line.

Although the postwar Burma Union did not suffer the agonies of a colonial war, as did French Indochina and Dutch Indonesia, its history since independence has been a troubled one. The Burmese political elite inherited from the colonial period a limited but valuable experience in the operations of British parliamentary institutions, and Premier Nu made a brave attempt to popularize democratic principles. He was severely handicapped during the first several years of independence, from 1948 to 1951, by civil strife; but he also failed to improve subsequent opportunities afforded him to establish an effective constitutional regime. Even though the principle of popular sovereignty was applied in repeated election campaigns, it aroused no understanding response within the context of alien Burmese political traditions. Premier Nu also attempted to qualify personally as a ruler in the traditional sense through his patronage of Buddhist revival and by his sharing of popular regard for associated animistic practices. He simply could not bring himself to exercise vigorously and effectively the power which his repeated election victories accorded him. Part of the trouble stemmed from the fact that his position as "king" was not authenticated in the popular mind by occupancy of sacred palace premises and by possession of the sacred sword and the white umbrella symbols of divine kingship. His government failed to implement a feasible program of economic development, to re-establish orderly administrative procedures free from local political interference, or even to resolve differences on policy and personal grounds within its own ranks.

In retrospect, Premier Nu clearly staked too much on his persistent efforts to stimulate a religious revival. His most dramatic move was to convene the Sixth Great Theravada Buddhist Council at Rangoon from 1954 to 1956. Although the 1947 Constitution of U Aung San had been strictly secular, Premier Nu committed himself to what he regarded as the supremely meritorious objective of making Burma a Buddhist state. Nu's efforts to promote the cause of religion came to grief mainly because they were not accompanied by measures designed to establish a modicum of discipline within the somewhat demoralized and politically ambitious elements of the Sangha. Premier Nu was more inclined on public occasions to dispense homilies on honesty and piety than to tackle pressing problems of order and economic development. His demonstrated popularity in winning successive elections probably owed as much to his easygoing habits as to his presumed embodiment of the Emergent Buddha, or *Bodhisattva*, ideal or his actual ability to command respect and obedience. Similarly, Premier Nu's attempt to keep himself in power in 1958 by soliciting the support of ethnic minorities by promising them substantial measures of autonomy threatened in time to disrupt the Union. The poorly integrated Anti-Fascist Peoples Freedom League (AFPFL) coalition broke up in May 1958, largely over divergent interests and personal rivalries.

Burma's history after 1958 witnessed a persistent transition toward army control. The army first took over power as a caretaker regime in the fall of 1958 with consent of rival political factions as a means of preserving governmental authority and preventing the outbreak of civil war. It accomplished many useful things during the sixteen months of caretaker rule, but basic problems remained unsolved and most elements of Burmese society grew tired of arbitrarily imposed army discipline. New elections were staged in early 1960, fulfilling promises previously given by the army. Nu's party was returned to office with a larger majority than ever, but at a heavy price. Nu promised religious partisans that he would transform Burma into a Buddhist state, and he also agreed to consider autonomy demands of important minority groups such as the Mons, Shans, Kachins, and the Arakanese. The Premier, in his second chance, proved to be no better an administrator than before. The enactment of several proposed religious amendments fomented communal rioting led by undisciplined younger members of the Sangha monkhood, and his negotiations with minority elements threatened, in the view of army leaders, to disrupt the Union.

A second army takeover, engineered in early March 1962, brushed aside the entire pattern of constitutional government. Army leaders affirmed the self-appointed role of the military as the preserver of the Burma state and the promoter of socialist revolution. In contrast to the cautious approach which had characterized the first caretaker regime, General Ne Win inaugurated a thoroughgoing program of planned social development, which was designed also to prevent profiteering by private employers and to lower consumer prices.

One of the first moves of the new government was to cancel

private export and import licenses, previously much abused, and to utilize profits from overseas trade to acquire needed production facilities. Private merchants, largely aliens, and government-sponsored Cooperatives and Civil Supply Shops were replaced by registered Peoples Stores, which were required to sell at minimal mark-ups so that consumer prices could be reduced. The system was later abandoned because flagrant abuses developed from the practice of queuing up at such shops for products in short supply and reselling the items to blackmarket operators. In 1963 a complete monopoly was imposed in government shops to cover the sale of food, textiles, and general merchandise in domestic trade, plus the nationalization of all warehouse and wholesale operations, banking and brokerage services, and timber depots. Army officers headed such commercial facilities, and only Burmese nationals were encouraged to seek employment therein. Nationalized firms were obliged to turn over business facilities and goods inventories on a promise of reasonable compensation, but they were still liable for old debts. Army inspection teams supervised the functioning of the new agencies. These measures meant the virtual abolition of private business activity in major commodity areas and produced a mass exodus of Indian and Pakistani businessmen. State revenues were realized from participation in trade, both foreign and domestic, and from an improved system of income tax collection.

The principal emphasis in economic development under Ne Win's army regime was placed on the agricultural sector, which had been neglected by Premier Nu's governments. The authorities set up several thousand rural and agricultural banking agencies to channel credits to peasant producers and to see that such loans were spent for productive ends. Special emphasis was placed on fertilization, land reclamation, and improved cultivation methods and seed quality. Rebels who surrendered were promised ten-acre plots, and foreign experts in both wet and dry farming were brought in from Israel, Japan, and Thailand. Printed handbooks describing better farming methods, including pest control and animal husbandry, were widely distributed. Tractors were purchased from France and Eastern European countries, and training stations were established to educate Burmans in their proper maintenance. Old embankments for flood control were repaired and new ones built; an estimated 800,000 acres of new canal-irrigated land were brought under cultivation within two years' time. Peasant seminars afforded opportunity for airing grievances and for discussing basic problems. Because of defaulted payments, drastic reductions in the amount of peasant loans came in 1963, a move which produced complaints but no organized resistance.

The "Burmese Road to Socialism" as devised by Ne Win's Revolutionary Council was agriculturally oriented, but not in the direction of land communization.

The army government's declared economic objective was to establish a united and prosperous Burma. The new order was to be based on regional and ethnic equality and was dedicated to the elimination of predatory bureaucrats and capitalists and to the improvement of the living standards of worker and peasant groups. In the industrial development sector, preference was given to facilities needed for the processing of agricultural output, such as cotton gins and textile mills, the extraction of cooking oils, sugar refining, and the manufacture of gunny sacks. Other economic emphases included electrical energy production, oil extraction and refining, increased mineral and timber output, and fishing activities. Nevertheless, during the four years since the army takeover in 1962, economic progress has been painfully slow, despite continued Japanese reparations aid, help from the Colombo Plan funds, and Chinese assistance in the form of a loan of eighty-one million dollars, plus the construction of several industrial plants. Although popular resistance has not been coordinated, the slow rate of economic progress has helped undermine the prestige of the army regime.

Burma's Revolutionary Council, headed by Ne Win, has also failed politically in its attempt to enlist support from articulate elements of the population. General Ne Win's efforts to organize a monolithic Revolutionary Program Party were as fruitless as were his subsequent negotiations in 1963 to reconcile various rebel factions. By the end of 1963, the military regime was reduced to the employment of naked power in the implementation of its political and economic policies. The government imprisoned not only its political opponents but also its critics in the business community and the press. When hostile student agitation flared in November 1963, Rangoon University was closed down completely for a full year. It was reopened in late 1964 on a restricted basis as to both membership and curriculum, with the new program carrying a strong Marxist tinge. Popular acceptance of Ne Win's regime has been withheld partly because the government lacks both the traditional symbols of authority and postwar constitutional sanctions, and partly because it repudiated Nu's previous establishment of a Buddhist state. Apart from the army itself, all major elements of Burma's elite have been alienated, including civil servants, labor leaders and the business community, teachers and student leaders, Buddhist monks, book and film distributors, and the press. Although the coalescence of such restive factions has been successfully forestalled, the heavy involvement of army leadership in political and economic responsibilities has limited the regime's capacity to curb overt rebellion among ethnic minority groups. One Karen faction was temporarily pacified, but rebel-bandit gangs roam unchecked in the eastern Shan plateau, while the Kachin independence movement in the extreme north has only been softened by appeasement.

Burma's military dictatorship, with one exception only, has reduced international contacts to a minimum, including importation of books and tourist visits. All nonpublic American relations were cut off, including the generally constructive Asia and Ford Foundation programs and even grants by the Fulbright Foundation. The one exception has been Communist China, whose Foreign Minister, Chou En-lai, has become a frequent if sometimes uninvited visitor to Rangoon. General Ne Win's emphatic advocacy of a thoroughgoing system of state socialism to the virtual exclusion of private business activity apparently constitutes, among other things, a direct bid for Peking's approval. Even so, Burma's alignment with Red China is something less than complete. The influential official Chinese bank at Rangoon was nationalized along with those of the West. Rangoon's apparent condoning of Chinese aggression against India was qualified on the occasion of the state visit of party chairman Liu Shao-chi, in April 1963, by the exaction of a promise that China would seek a peaceful settlement of the Indian frontier problem. Ne Win's government also departed from China's example by signing the nuclear test ban treaty and by refusing to sign a joint denunciation with China of United States policy in Vietnam. Ne Win has also complained sharply about continued Chinese propaganda support of the no longer significant Communist rebellion in Burma. On the other hand, Ne Win refused to protest Viet Minh interventions in both Laos and South Vietnam and rejected abruptly Delhi's objections to Burma's spoliation and exclusion of some 3,000,000 Indians, including professionals and businessmen. Burma's brand of neutralism continues to have a xenophobic ring similar to the isolationist traditions of monarchial times.

Postwar Thailand

As a state which maintained its independent identity in opposition to threatened colonial control, Siam (as it was known prior to 1939) had far more experience than its neighbors in making political adjustments to the outside world. Its traditional policy in modern times was to "bend with the wind" by keeping on good terms with the

strongest outside power impinging on the area. Prior to the mid-
nineteenth century, this power was China; from the 1850s to the
1930s, it was Britain and British India; in the late 1930s, Siam's
orientation shifted toward an ascendant Japan; and since 1945,
Bangkok has been closely associated with the United States.

The pro-American orientation at Bangkok began during the later
phases of World War II under the leadership of the civilian-
sponsored Free Thai government, which assumed control at Bangkok
in the summer of 1944 when it became apparent that Japan was
losing the war. The Free Thai government was led by the Leftist-
inclined Thai politician, Pridi Phonomyong, and by the conservative
Thai ambassador to Washington, Prince Seni Promoj. The latter
simply refused to deliver to the State Department Bangkok's 1942
declaration of war against the United States, discounting it as un-
representative of the wishes of the Thai people. Pridi established
intelligence contacts with Allied headquarters in Ceylon in 1943 and
prepared during the ensuing two years to assist Allied efforts in the
eventual defeat of the Japanese. Although Thai military assistance
was destined never to be utilized, Washington felt justified in ignoring
Marshal Pibun's declaration of war, and in objecting to punitive
aspects of postwar British demands made on Bangkok. Washington
did demand that Thailand's wartime territorial gains, achieved
through Japanese support, be surrendered. America subsequently
supported Thailand's entry into the United Nations, and the State
Department's newly organized Southeast Asia Policy Division, which
was permitted a free hand only in fashioning Thailand policies,
fostered increasingly cordial relations.

Both before the war and since, Bangkok resisted the influence of
China in its domestic affairs. This policy became related to Thai
nationalism, and after 1932 the linguistic and political assimilation
of the two to three million resident Chinese was attempted with
some success. The Chinese proved, however, unassailably strong in
the economic sphere, in the absence of deliberately applied governmental interference. Communist victory in China in 1949 provided
an added reason for strengthening American-Thai cooperation. This
friendship eventually found expression in the SEATO alliance of
September 1954, following the French military debacle at Dienbienphu and the increasingly aggressive Communist Viet Minh
intervention in neighboring Laos. Thailand's membership in SEATO
served also to strengthen the political control of the dominant military
faction in Thailand's government, that of Pibun and Phao from 1947
and, after 1957, that of Marshal Sarit Thanarat. Additional and

effective unilateral assurances were forthcoming from America after 1961 to cover the security of Thailand's Laotian border area. An additional but minor factor in the problem of worsening Thai-Chinese relations was the role of the exiled Pridi as a refugee in Red China, where he was encouraged after 1949 to revive his Free Thai movement in Yunnan under radically different auspices from those of World War II.

Other than the close relations between ruling groups in Thailand and conservative military elements in Laos, Bangkok's postwar relations with its encircling Buddhist neighbors have not been particularly cordial. Labored efforts to promote friendly relations with Burma on the basis of cultural exchanges have been moderately successful. But Rangoon has been inclined, since 1953, to cultivate friendly relations with China and to regard Thailand's close cooperation with the United States as gratuitously provocative of cold war involvement for all peoples of peninsular Southeast Asia. Difficulties developing along the Burma-Thailand border have included the control of Kuomintang refugees, Karen rebel intrusions into Thailand, opium smuggling, and the incursions of Thai fishermen into Burmese waters near Victoria Point in the extreme south. Fortunately, these problems have so far been amenable to peaceful settlement, the convention negotiated in March 1963 between Thailand and Burma being a case in point.

Thailand's postwar relations with Cambodia have been especially bad since 1954. Aside from territorial disputes carrying over from Thailand's wartime annexations of Khmer territories, the two neighbors have adopted divergent attitudes with regard to the cold war. Bangkok has alleged that the brand of "neutralism" espoused by Cambodia's Prince Norodom Sihanouk has actually opened up all of Southeast Asia to Communist infiltration, both Chinese and Viet Minh. Thai authorities accorded very grudging consent to the settlement by the World Court in Cambodia's favor of the 1962 Preah Vihear frontier temple dispute mentioned above. In response to the apparent hostility of Bangkok, the authorities at Phnom Penh have responded in kind. Prince Sihanouk has denounced American efforts to bolster Thailand's military deterrent against potential Communist aggression via Laos as directly endangering Cambodia's security. Some observers feel, however, that if Bangkok should ever conclude that Washington was wavering in its determination to check Communist expansion in Southeast Asia, Thailand would itself most likely undertake to make some kind of accommodation with China following the example of Burma.

During most of the time since 1932, when the modernizing

"promoters" at Bangkok set aside the arbitrary rule of the Siamese king, the army has dominated the government. The succession of constitutions operative in Thailand from 1932 to 1951 and from 1955 to 1958 amounted to little more than a façade designed to impress Western observers. Governmental coups at Bangkok, occurring on the average of three or four times per decade, invariably saw one element of the political elite supplanting another in a game of musical chairs. The process apparently concerned the people of the countryside very little. Since the army constituted the best-organized political clique, its representatives managed to exercise control. In 1951, Field Marshal Pibun dissolved the legislature and reverted to pre-1946 standards of *de facto* army control, but the idea of representative government refused to die. Pibun restored full constitutional procedures in 1955 long enough to stage two rounds of elections in 1957, the last of which went against him. A rival military faction gained control, led by Marshal Sarit Thanarat, who installed General Thanom Kittikachorn to act as Premier for the better part of a year. Sarit himself assumed direct dictatorial control in October 1958, again dissolving the National Assembly and abrogating the constitution. In establishing his own monopolistic Revolutionary party, the Thai dictator set a pattern which Burma's General Ne Win eventually attempted to copy in 1962, but with less success. The desire for constitutional government was nevertheless reaffirmed following Sarit's death in December 1963 by his successor Prime Minister Thanom Kittikachorn.

Despite these periodic coups staged in the capital, Thailand's government has maintained a remarkable degree of administrative stability. This may be attributed mainly to the fact that the permanent bureaucracy has continued to function with unimpaired authority. Another contributory factor is that King Bhumibol Adulyadej holds the respect and admiration of the Thai people. He also possessed the white umbrella and the sacred sword, the traditional symbols of divine kingship which have retained vitality in the popular consciousness. The National Assembly, although precariously maintained until 1958 and far from democratic, served a useful political role in affording opportunity for recognition and expression of provincial leadership as distinct from the cliques dominating the Bangkok scene. Thailand's greater administrative and cultural stability, as compared to that of post-war Burma, also owed much to Siam's having escaped the disruptive aspects of colonial rule. As a result basic social and governmental institutions remained intact. Thailand's postwar government suffered, nevertheless, from erosion of official responsibility and from the decline in the moral standards of the ruling elite. Few officials escaped the general corruption of the governmental services, and the opium traffic provided a particularly potent temptation.

Thailand's postwar economic development and population growth surpassed that of any of its neighbors, owing in part to its avoidance of military destruction during the war and in part to substantial financial aid from the outside. Gains in heavy industry and transportation were realized largely through government initiative, but the private sector was also active. Bank deposits doubled between 1955 and 1962, providing funds for expanding commercial credit needs. Foreign investment was encouraged to enter the economy in various areas of unsatisfied consumer demand. The official Board of Investment accorded potential investors a five-year income tax holiday, plus waiver of import duties on machinery and raw material needs. Private Thai production increased substantially despite the competition of Japanese goods, the expressions of jealousy by army-directed firms, and the inordinate amount of paper work required of foreign investors. Marshal Sarit projected a comprehensive six-year development plan, which was supplemented by well-conceived regional programs for the development of the Korat plateau near the Laos border and of the Mekong valley generally. These programs included irrigation projects, roads, power installations, communication facilities, and vocational institutes in engineering and agriculture.

Postwar Thailand has succeeded in its efforts for economic development partly because social and governmental stability afforded the requisite time and leadership, and partly because the Westernized orientation of the political elite extended backward in time over a full century. As head of the key Ministry of National Development over a five-year period, Premier Marshal Sarit won for himself an impressive reputation for economic accomplishment. He also acted to clean up Bangkok's streets and canals, and attempted to curb the opium-smoking evil along with various forms of graft and vice. He also collaborated politically with his Laos cousin, General Phoumi Nosavan, the American-supported Rightist leader. Damaging revelations which came to light following Sarit's death in late 1963 concerning his own irregular marital relations and heavy personal and family involvement in corruption did much to besmirch the image of his public career. He and his family amassed an enormous fortune through the ownership of shares in some thirty state-sponsored business enterprises. The fact remained, nevertheless, that Thailand was prospering in spite of manifold political and economic irregularities connected with army control and state-planned development.

Following the death of Marshal Sarit in December 1963, the Deputy Premier, Marshal Thanom Kittikachorn, took over control in what appeared at the time as a temporary expedient. Profiting from the fact that some of his political rivals were implicated in the Sarit scandal, General Thanom Kittikachorn, with the aid of strongman General Prapas Charusathien, has maintained his control and won respect through a demonstration of personal integrity and effectiveness. Among other actions, he reactivated the committee previously assigned to work out a revision of the pre-1958 constitution and has proposed to hold new elections. The new constitution will reportedly provide for an elected lower house, an appointive upper chamber, and a Cabinet responsible to the popular King Bhumbol Adulyadej. Whether the constitutional government is actually revived as planned appears to depend upon the decision of the army leadership concerning the probable domestic and international consequences. Political developments in Laos and in the Korat plateau area adjacent to Laos will doubtless be major considerations in this decision.

Revival of Cambodian Independence

Cambodia's postwar relations with its immediate neighbors and with regard to world alignments were fashioned almost entirely by Prince Norodom Sihanouk, first as King and later as Prince-Premier and political boss. The ephemeral Japanese-sponsored Free Khmer movement led by Son Ngoc Thanh, which was set up at the end of World War II, was ousted without serious difficulty by returning French General Le Clerc in October 1945. Son Ngoc Thanh escaped to anti-French Thailand for a time, but eventually led a portion of his Free Khmer following into a more vigorous anti-imperialist collaboration sponsored by Viet Minh agents. The original French political concession to King Sihanouk's seemingly pliant regime, made in January 1946, pledged self-government for Cambodia within the French Union, but it left the colonial authorities in control of all economic activities and all important governmental operations. The King, in 1953, blackmailed the French into granting substantial additional concessions by simply going into temporary exile in Thailand. Cambodia's independence was fully acknowledged by the Geneva settlement of 1954, following the French military debacle at Dienbienphu. King Norodom Sihanouk emerged as a national hero.

The French withdrawal nevertheless posed a frightening prospect for Cambodia, both domestically and internationally. Cambodia faced traditionally hostile neighbors on both sides, while political agitators, acting partly under Free Khmer and partly under Viet Minh instigation, threatened internal peace. In order to meet these challenges in the political and diplomatic arenas, King Sihanouk took the drastic step in 1955 of abdicating in favor of his father and assuming the role of Premier and political boss. The task was far from easy, but the Prince's leadership was effectively exerted in the domestic sphere.

The Prince-Premier's domestic role as a politician, meanwhile, was both bold and effective. Despairing of achieving his desire for authoritarian government in the face of fairly strong Democratic party opposition, he at first postponed the holding of elections and then proceeded in 1955 to fashion his own patriotic party, which he called the People's Socialist Community (Sangkum). By exerting pressure on a variety of political elements, he managed to achieve an overwhelming victory for the Sangkum in the election of September 1955. In order to mold to his liking the amorphous and rivalry-ridden Sangkum majority, he later convened a series of semiannual National Congresses, town-meeting style. Participants in the Congresses were selected from every social stratum by the Sangkum directorate, and the sessions convened under the King's personal chairmanship. They provided a forum for the airing of popular grievances and policy proposals, occasionally calling the Ministers themselves to account.

Beginning in 1958, the Prince-Premier, turned party boss, took a further step by appointing a special Commission to select the candidates for election within the Sangkum party. Acting on Sihanouk's orders, the Commission gave preference to the European-educated youthful elite, whose training and abilities the Prince apparently wished to exploit and whose potential opposition leadership he obviously desired to circumvent. In the 1958 election, the vote for the well-regulated Sangkum party was virtually one hundred per cent. Two years later, Prince Norodom Sihanouk, acting according to the time-honored French pattern, engineered by plebiscite his own elevation to the permanent post of Chief of State. Postwar Cambodia has thus been completely dominated by Prince Norodom Sihanouk, albeit with the apparent consent of an overwhelming majority of the population.

The United States from the outset contributed generously to the economic and security needs of Cambodia following its attainment of independence in 1954. The total American contribution of some $275 millions of aid, accorded from 1954 to 1963, included consumer goods, capital equipment, and military supplies. Additional special grants of around $88 millions were made for education, public health, agriculture, and transportation. Two-thirds of the counterpart funds realized from the sale of American-provided consumer goods were assigned to the country's defense budget. The aid program came to an end in 1963 on the initiative of Prince Norodom. He accused the United States of arming Cambodia's enemies and of countenancing threats to Cambodia's security from neighboring South Vietnam and Thailand. At the time, Sihanouk expressed the hope that France might be ready to fill the aid gap so created. France had already contributed to the new airport at Phnom Penh and to the new seaport of Sihanoukville. American engineers built the costly mountain road connecting the port with the capital.

Aid from France eventually ran aground over a number of economic differences. They involved the nationalization of French banks in December 1963, compensation for the seizure of some 42,000 hectares of French-owned rubber plantations, and disputes concerning the value to be placed on the French franc. France continued to support Cambodia's neutralist policy and to provide military instructors and educational assistance throughout much of 1964. In October 1964, Sihanouk finally declared that French as well as American assistance was imperialist influenced and, therefore, no longer acceptable. Meanwhile Cambodia's relations with the United States and with South Vietnam reached a near breaking point as a result of border incidents involving the activities of Viet Cong rebels.

As a substitute for American and French assistance, Prince Norodom undertook to ingratiate himself with the rival Communist bloc. He became convinced, as early as 1955-56 that the cultivation of good relations with the leading states of Eastern Asia would serve Cambodia's future interests, especially in view of the probable ephemeral role of the United States. He started first with Japan and Nationalist China in 1955, but during the course of the following year modulated over to the cultivation of the Peking and Hanoi regimes and the Soviet Union. He apparently reasoned that the two great Communist powers, if friendly to Cambodia, could restrain the disruptive activities of Viet Minh agents within his own country and that they would be able to contribute substantial aid to supplement, if not to displace, that of the United States and France. He argued openly that the preservation of his country's political independence was worth the risks involved in a pro-Chinese Communist diplomatic orientation, even though he admitted that Cambodia itself might turn Communist in the process. Once started along the road, he discovered that the price of good relations with China was to exclude both American and French influence, but he managed with some skill to play both sides of the street for some time.

To counteract United States influence in particular, Communist countries agreed to contribute substantial economic assistance to Cambodia. From China, Sihanouk obtained the installation of a plywood factory, a paper mill, a textile factory, and the promise of a cement works. Communist Czechoslovakia agreed to finance on generous terms a sugar refinery, a tire factory, and a tractor assembly plant. Soviet negotiators offered to contribute a hospital, hotel facilities, and a technical institute. Some difficulties were encountered in the operation and maintenance of such a congeries of industrial installations, but Cambodia's bid for assistance from both sides paid off handsomely in terms of visible economic progress. The drift in the direction of accommodation with Red China gained momentum during the period of political confusion following the assassination of Ngo Dinh Diem in the fall of 1963. By mid-1964, Cambodia found itself virtually dependent on Communist Chinese assistance both economically and militarily. Following an eight-day visit in Peking in October 1964, Prince Norodom declared that Cambodia and China were "brothers in arms" and boasted that United States imperialism would never be able to separate the two. Peking responded a month later by pledging full military support against alleged American threats to Cambodia's independence. The final move into alignment with the China camp, later in 1964, was Phnom Penh's recognition of the Viet Minh–Viet Cong regimes in neighboring Vietnam and the Chinese-supported regime of North Korea. Cambodia thus paid homage to fate.

The popular regime of Cambodia's princely Chief of State, as of 1966, reflected an aura of progress which was far from real. Underneath the show of material gains, such as an airport, a highway, public buildings, and factories, persisted much of the traditional order. The Khmers characteristically kept their sense of humor and were not greatly concerned politically. The nationalization of trade pinched the resident Chinese more than the indigenous population or the Europeans. For the 7,000 French residents, food and lodging were becoming very expensive, and the diminishing supply of luxury goods was priced virtually out of reach. The French presence in Cambodia was still felt culturally, but nine new Chinese newspapers subservient to Peking overshadowed the two remaining French ones. Imports were declining in volume, and prices were rising. Even though coupon money was available at half price for visitors to Angkor Wat, the tourist trade was limited to a small fraction of its potential. With all of Sihanouk's paraded pro-Chinese orientation, the government still employed French military and technical advisers and sent selected overseas students to France rather than to China for training.

Laos Since 1945

In the backward and artificial state of Laos, where only one per cent of the population possessed an elementary education, postwar politics tended to crystallize around the ambitions of princely rivals. Some deference was paid to the authority of the King at Luang Prabang, but genuine nationalist sentiment was lacking. The royal Court at Luang Prabang acquiesced at first in the restoration of French control as a means of preserving the monarchy and the nation's identity. In accord with this policy, Prince Boun Oum of the southern province of Champassak welcomed the return of French forces to his area in late 1945. The restoration of French control also seemed particularly desirable in the north as a means of getting rid of the looting Chinese armies present at Allied invitation, ostensibly to accept the surrender of the already departed Japanese. The unwelcome Chinese forces finally retired in June 1946, as a result of an agreement reached with French authorities.

Meanwhile, an anti-French Free Lao faction (*Lao Issara*) established temporary control at Vientiane, the French colonial administrative center, distinct from the royal Court located at Luang Prabang. The *Lao Issara* was a heterogeneous coterie led by frustrated princely politicians and other disgruntled personalities. Some of them were nationalists associated with the Communist-led Viet Minh movement centering in Tongking. When the returning French army reoccupied both Vientiane and Luang Prabang without difficulty in the spring of 1946, a number of the princes took refuge with other *Lao Issara* partisans in Thailand, itself also strongly anti-French. French proposals made verbally to Laotian authorities in 1946, including the promise of an autonomous and unified country, and the subsequent convening of a constituent assembly in early 1947, prepared the way for the restoration of a modified form of colonial rule.

In a formal convention of July 1949, France recognized the independence of Laos within the French Union under King Sisavang Vong. Although the final negotiation of agreements defining more precisely the status of Laotian relations with France, Vietnam, and Cambodia was postponed awaiting the hoped-for end of the Viet Minh rebellion, the 1949 convention was sufficiently satisfactory to most of the politically ambitious Free Lao leaders to provide a basis for their return under amnesty guarantees. By 1953, the former exiles occupied a majority of the seven Ministerships. Prince Boun Oum became President of the King's Council and Inspector-General for life within his Champassak province.

The principal Laotian malcontent holdouts were the sulking ex-Viceroy in charge of the military, Prince Phetsarath, who had made himself *persona non grata* to the King, and his able half-brother, Prince Souphanouvong. The latter prince, who was married to a Vietnamese Communist, became the head of a "Liberation Committee" maintaining political connections with the Viet Minh and backing a new Pathet Lao (Lao Country) movement. This Pathet Lao movement succeeded the *Lao Issara*, which had disbanded in 1949. Following the eventual collapse of the French military effort at Dienbienphu in the spring of 1954, Prince Souphanouvong's Pathet Lao Liberation group received substantial support from the victorious Viet Minh authorities. The prince also enlisted successfully the co-operation of restive hill tribesmen, especially from the Kha in the south, who resented traditional Laotian domination. The Pathet Lao maintained its own political identity and managed to exercise *de facto* control over two Laotian provinces bordering Tongking pending accomplishment of a formal political settlement between the princely rivals.

Negotiations for a political settlement in Laos first ran aground in 1955 over disagreement regarding the status of Pathet Lao representatives to be included within the government. The Pathet Lao faction was accordingly permitted no share in the 1955 elections. A tentative agreement was finally reached in late 1956 between the princely half-brothers, Souvanna Phouma and Souphanouvong. It committed the government to pursue a neutralist policy internationally and permitted the Pathet Lao to function as a recognized political party in the supplementary elections, which were later staged, for additional National Assembly seats. The Pathet leaders agreed in turn to place their troops under royal command and to turn over their two frontier provinces.

Further difficulties were encountered, however, in executing the 1956 agreement, difficulties which were attributable in part to outside Communist pressure. Premier Souvanna Phouma accordingly visited both Hanoi and Peking in an effort to expedite an understanding. He realized a measure of success in late 1957, when nominal central government control of the two border provinces was actually attained. Pathet Lao's Souphanouvong was granted at the time the post of Minister of Economic Planning and one of his subordinates was made Minister of Religion, a key position for influencing Buddhist opinion. However, friction again developed on several issues. The ambitious planning program prepared by Prince Souphanouvong for agriculture, industry, and social services proved completely unrealistic both financially and technologically, especially in view of prevailing problems of disorder and corruption. The Pathet Lao faction also objected strongly to American efforts to develop and equip the royalist army. Another major factor of difficulty concerned the unfortunate tendency on Washington's part to view the local political situation exclusively in terms of the cold war.

Overt American interference in Laos began in 1958 on two fronts. The first involved a substantial effort to halt the scandalous and debilitating speculation by favored persons in American-provided import license dollars. Manipulators in high positions shifted the prices of holdings of licensed imports from dollars to *kip* and back to dollars at regular and black market rates of exchange, waxing opulent from such tactics. The aid program was thus robbed of well over half of its funds. In order to force the acceptance of a more realistic exchange rate as an essential step in halting such speculation, the United States was obliged to suspend aid entirely for four months in mid-1958. A second American policy undertook after 1956 to develop a more effective Laotian fighting force. Ordinary recruits could be attracted into the army by the relatively high pay, but as soldiers they demonstrated little desire to accept discipline or to prepare themselves for actual combat. In an attempt to develop an elite fighting corps, the American Central Intelligence Agency sponsored the creation of a youthful patriotic force headed by an anti-Communist "Committee of Defense of the National Interest." The body was led by General Phoumi Nosavan, a youthful associate of Prince Boun Oum of Champassak and an ardent Rightist. In the end both of these U.S. policy efforts brought unfortunate results.

The prime casualty of the American intervention, whether so intended or not, was the collapse of the neutralist coalition headed by Prince Souvanna Phouma and the consequent veto of any political settlement with the Pathet Lao faction led by Souphanouvong. The successor government under Premier Sananikone, which took over in June 1958, was thoroughly anti-Communist in its orientation, but it proved woefully ineffective and not really amenable to American reforming influence. When in late 1958, Pathet Lao guerrilla operations were resumed, American financial support for the government had to be substantially increased, until it covered an estimated nine-tenths of the entire budget for civilian administration, police, and the military. Premier Sananikone tried unsuccessfully to involve the United States even more deeply in Laotian affairs by circulating unsubstantiated scare stories concerning wholesale invasion on the part of Viet Minh Communist forces. Official corruption revived on a still larger scale.

The downfall of the faltering Sananikone regime in December 1959, was accomplished through political and military pressure from the Rightist General Phoumi Nosavan and his C.I.A.-sponsored anti-Communist Defense Committee organization. Once in control, the General imprisoned Prince Souphanouvong and other Pathet Lao leaders and then, in April 1960, staged rigged National Assembly elections. This high-handed regime was disrupted four months later, in August 1960, by the seizure of Vientiane by the neutralist leader Captain Kong Lê, a half-Kha nationalist paratrooper commander who had been driven by the Rightist coup into alliance with the Left. His action came at a time when most of the princely governmental leaders were attending the coronation of the new King Savang Vatthana at Luang Prabang. Kong Lê demanded an end of civil strife and the cessation of American interference in Laos. His action brought eventual American acquiescence in the restoration of the neutralist Premier Souvanna Phouma, who undertook to revive the previously aborted efforts to reach a political settlement with the Pathet Lao. Meanwhile, the imprisoned Pathet Lao leaders escaped from jail and began actively to prepare for the resumption of expanded guerrilla operations. For obvious reasons, Americans became discouraged.

Things continued to go badly. King Savang Vatthana disliked Souvanna Phouma personally, and American advisers eventually demonstrated their own hostility to Souvanna's conciliatory policy by suspending economic aid for a brief period. In December 1960, the American-supplied forces of General Phoumi Nosavan, moving up from the south, again captured Vientiane, forcing Captain Kong Lê's forces to withdraw northward and obliging Souvanna Phouma to seek temporary refuge in Cambodia. The Rightist government headed by General Phoumi and Prince Boun Oum was promptly accepted by the King.

The new Rightist regime proved to be decidedly ineffective, even though strongly supported by both the Americans and by Thai authorities. Kong Lê's refugees began cooperating with the Pathet Lao guerrillas, who were for a time accorded ample support in essential military supplies airlifted from the Soviet Union via North Vietnam. As was finally demonstrated in the spring of 1961, the American-supplied royalist troops, when placed in actual confrontation with Pathet Lao–Viet Minh forces in the vicinity of Luang Prabang, had no heart for a showdown fight. Another development coming to light at this time was that during General Phoumi Nosavan's period of prominence from 1960 to 1963, he had developed a lucrative chain of gambling casinos, had controlled all liquor and perfume imports, and had used the gold monopoly of the Bank of Laos for smuggling precious metal out of the country, all at great profit to himself. Thus American support of the anti-Communist Committee under General Phoumi worked to cancel out all efforts to eliminate official corruption and also failed to improve the military potential. After such discouraging experiences, the American government, unwilling to commit itself to direct military intervention, decided to settle for a neutralized Laos under a coalition government headed again by the twice rejected Prince Souvanna Phouma.

The prospects for effective neutralization of Laos were at first far from promising. De facto military authority within the country was polarized between the pro-Communist Pathet Lao forces and the Rightist armies of the King and General Phoumi Nosavan. The position of the neutralist Premier was decidedly weaker than it had been in 1958, which American intervention had first obliged him to retire. The only military forces directly loyal to Prince-Premier Souvanna Phouma were Captain Kong Lê's single battalion of paratroopers. The royal army contributed little or no support to Kong Lê's efforts to stem the revived Pathet Lao offensive. A flicker of hope developed in 1961, when Laos became a significant pawn in the Peking-Moscow chess game for leadership of the world Communist movement. Following the debacle of the Phoumi coup of 1959-60, Moscow assisted the American efforts to re-establish a neutral government at Vientiane by discontinuing the airlift of military supplies to North Vietnam and by bringing diplomatic pressure to bear on Hanoi authorities. A further relaxation of Washington-Moscow tension developed as a sequel to the perilous Cuban crisis of 1962-63. The Soviet Union was concerned that a general war not develop over a region as unimportant as was Laos to the interests of Moscow.

Taking a contrary point of view, Peking saw in the Laos situation, despite its lack of intrinsic importance, a chance to embarrass both Russian and American authorities and to establish a dominant position for China in North Vietnam. Active Viet Minh intervention in the affairs of both Laos and South Vietnam was accordingly encouraged by China. The situation assumed an ominous character in early 1962, when Viet Minh forces stepped up their support of Pathet

Lao attacks on the neutralist forces of Kong Lê. The threatening move was halted only by the temporary introduction of American forces into Thailand adjacent to the Laos border. The Viet Minh succeeded nevertheless in establishing effective control over the western slopes of the Annamite watershed, a position which facilitated Hanoi's increasing involvement in support of the Viet Cong Liberation Front of South Vietnam. The U.S.S.R. could not effectively express its concern over the unwanted prospect of a United States-Chinese confrontation in Southeast Asia because of Peking's jibes that Moscow was abandoning the world Communist revolution, and as a result Moscow lost considerable influence at Hanoi. After retaliatory bombing attacks by American carrier planes on North Vietnam shore installations following the Tongking Bay incident of August 1964, followed by further escalation of the war in 1965, the Russians were unable to continue their policy of restraint on Hanoi. The reported presence of Viet Minh agents in northwestern Thailand bent on promoting subversion at the village level involved additional and ominous implications for all of Southeast Asia.

Meanwhile, in Laos, the near collapse of the value of the *kip* currency in 1963 forced its second re-evaluation at 240 to the dollar, as compared to the previous 80 to the dollar. Even this new rate was less than half the black market price of the dollar. More than half of the imports entering Laos in 1963 were financed by American funds. Even so, there was little to show for the more than 450 million dollars of United States aid granted to Laos since 1954, of which some forty per cent had been allocated for military assistance. The corrupt administration of aid funds by Laotian officials had actually served to widen the gap between the Vientiane authorities and the Laos people generally.

A world-power struggle over Laos in particular and Southeast Asia in general did not develop, in part, because too little was at stake materially. The resources of Laos and its 2.4 million inhabitants could contribute virtually nothing to meet the needs of either North Vietnam or China in food or raw materials. In fact, China's acquisition of the entire surplus rice of both Thailand and the lower Mekong basin would provide only a small fraction of the deficit foods needs for 700 million people. Any Southeast Asian resources which China might use would have to be purchased and then transported by sea. Also clear was the fact that a second East Asian war triggered by any massive Chinese military intrusion into Southeast Asia, comparable to that of Japan in 1941-42, would be decided elsewhere than in the backward hill country of Laos. That country did afford, however, a fruitful theater for Communist activity following the French withdrawal in 1954 and the same was true subsequently in South Vietnam.

By the middle 1960s, the affairs of Southeast Asia had become a matter of important concern in world foreign policy. Laos and Thailand, along with Vietnam, were directly involved in the cold war rivalry, while Cambodia and Burma were seeking insurance against the resurgent power of Red China by trying to avoid offending Peking and by trying not to become involved in the threatening military confrontation. This habit of paying political deference to China's suzerainty while resisting actual Chinese control had a long tradition behind it in Southeast Asian countries. The neutralist policies pursued by Burma and Cambodia also afforded them the opportunity to solicit aid from both sides of the cold war. Any hope for peace in Southeast Asia seemed to turn precariously on the preference of both power blocs for neutralization as opposed to alignment of area countries with the opposing camp. America's postwar efforts to prevent Communist domination of the region had paid little heed to historical factors affecting the indigenous points of view of the countries involved. American policies also ran the risk of arousing local fears that an American protectorate against an alleged Communist threat might impair newly won independence. As we shall see, the history of Southeast Asian peoples had already inevitably conditioned their reactions to each other and to any form of external interference. It is to a consideration of such background data that the remainder of this monograph will be devoted.

TWO

HISTORICAL BEGINNINGS

Peoples and Migrations

The general trend of population movements in Indochina since prehistoric times has been from north to south in the direction of Malaya and the Indonesian islands. Four main avenues and several lesser ones were open for southward migration. The one farthest west, used by the Mons, the Pyu, and the Burmans, led down the Irrawaddy and Sittang valleys, and thence to the Tenasserim coast along the Bay of Bengal. Lower Burma could also be reached via the less convenient valley of the Salween River. A second route farther east led from the gorges of the upper Salween and Mekong Rivers into the tributaries of the Menam River of central Siam. From the lower Menam valley, the route proceeded down the eastern coast of the isthmus into Malaya. This route was used by the Malays, the Mons, and later by the Thai. A third route followed the Mekong valley down to the delta and westward into the basin of the Tonle Sap, or Great Lake, of Cambodia. Khmer peoples, proceeding via this route, were blocked from the sea for a time by Malayo-Polynesians and other peoples of Funan, while the Khmer in their turn held back the subsequently entering Lao and Thai peoples. A fourth avenue followed the narrow coastal littoral of Annam and moved southward, partly by sea, from Tongking toward the delta of the Mekong, pitting the eventually dominant Vietnamese against the Chams and latterly against the Khmers.

The leading ethnic groups of mainland Southeast Asia, the Malays, Vietnamese, Mons, Khmers, Pyu-Burmans, and the late-arriving Shan and Thai peoples all participated in turn in this southward migration, a movement which continued into modern times. Only the last group, the Thai, and the Vietnamese experienced any substantial contacts with Chinese civilization prior to their southward migration. The Vietnamese elite of Tongking and upper Annam became thoroughly Sinicized as a result of their country's thousand-year incorpora-

28

tion into China proper beginning in the late second century B.C. Aboriginal peoples included Negrito-Australoid and Veddoid groups, who are still found in scattered enclaves located in remote areas of forest and swamp. Several hundred distinct linguistic groups, culturally intermediate between the advanced peoples and the primitive peoples, survive as mountain tribesmen.

The first civilized inhabitants, the Malayo-Polynesians, proceeded down the peninsula in successive waves into Malaya and to the adjacent islands. The Funanese and Chams of historic times, and possibly the Vietnamese as well, constituted a kind of rear-guard element of this early population. All three borrowed elements of speech from the later arriving Khmers, and the Vietnamese also shared the tonal aspects of the speech of the Thai peoples, who long occupied interior areas adjacent to Tongking. The Chams controlled the lower Annam coastal region from the second century A.D. onward until they were finally eliminated politically by the Vietnamese in the fifteenth century. The Chams' simple Malayo-Polynesian language structure was refined by borrowings from the Khmers. The Proto-Malays of the northern part of the lower peninsula absorbed the political impact of the later-arriving Mons and Khmers, becoming in alternate periods vassals to both. The Proto-Malays also copied the Mon numeral system. Peninsular Malays lived as coastal and valley agriculturists and fishermen adjacent to remnants of aboriginal Negrito and Polynesian jungle dwellers, who were confined in historic times to the mountain areas and swamps.

The early peoples of Indochina, in Neolithic times prior to 2000 B.C., domesticated important food plants (yams, bananas, bread fruit, taro, and the like), along with the chicken, pig, and dog. After 2000 B.C. came developments in gardening, fruit tree growing, wet-rice cultivation, and the use of bronze tools, coupled with the utilization of the ox and the buffalo for plowing purposes. Hydraulic systems of irrigation, established mainly in delta regions, supplemented by systematic harvesting of fish protein foods from streams and coastal waters, provided essential food needs for the densely populated areas. Some of China's better strains of rice were borrowed from Southeast Asia. Hill tribesmen, by contrast, continued to live by food gathering and hunting, and by the cultivation of ever-shifting hillside clearings capable of producing meager food crops of vegetables and dry rice.

Topography and Ecology

Topography and climatic factors played a dominant role in the development of early centers of civilization in Indochina. The principal avenues of migration, previously described, were separated by mountainous watersheds running north and south which inhibited transverse communication. The boundary regions were inhabited by a great variety of hillside-cultivating tribesmen. The Chin and Naga ranges mark the historic boundary between Burma and India. The lower Irrawaddy valley was separated from the Arakan coast by the Yoma of the same name and from the parallel Sittang valley by the Pegu Yoma. Peripheral areas to the Irrawaddy delta were inhabited by Karen peoples, who were divided into three major language groups. Karen tribesmen also overflowed into the trans-Salween and Tenasserim mountains separating Burma from Siam. The mountains of the extreme northern parts of Burma were settled by a variety of Kachin tribesmen. The broad Shan plateau bordering the Sittang and upper Irrawaddy valleys extending to the east into north Siam and Laos contained a bewildering medley of linguistic groups. These groups were interspersed among the economically and politically dominant Shan wet-rice cultivators who occupied the more desirable agricultural areas. The frontier between the Menam and Mekong valleys, including the Korat plateau, was less rugged than the Shan plateau, and it came to be dominated successively by the Khmers and the Thai. It afforded, however, no substantial basis for developing political or economic power comparable to that of the lower river areas.

The situation was much the same to the east of the Mekong River. The cordillera separating the Mekong valley from coastal Tongking and Annam constituted a substantial barrier to transverse trade and population movement. Its southern reaches are still inhabited by Cham remnants and by some nine or ten varieties of primitive Khmer-speaking peoples known as the Moi in Annam and as the Kha in Laos and Cambodia. (*Kha* is the Lao and *Moi* the Annamese word for slave.) Other unclassified branches of the Kha, some sixteen all told, became widely scattered throughout hill areas of Northern Laos. Other hill tribesmen of Laos speak a version of the Thai language indigenous to Yunnan, China, and are similar in other respects to the Yunnan Chinese.

The lowland Mekong valley Lao are closely akin to the Thai of Siam in language, religious orientation, and traditional governmental forms, although the two have become somewhat differentiated culturally in modern times. Finally, the Cardaman mountain area of coastal Cambodia still contains Negrito survivors of an aboriginal population.

The differences between the politically dominant wet-rice cultivators of the lowlands and the more diverse shifting hillside-cultivator groups were partly ethnic but mainly ecological. The principal centers of political power developed around the larger delta areas and along major river tributaries. There the abundant rainfall of the summer monsoon winds (ranging from 60 inches to more than 200) and the annual sedimentation resulting from flooding provided ample resources for wet-rice cultivation. The widely dispersed summer monsoon rainfall (excepting only several rainshadow areas) failed for several reasons to provide suitable conditions for general agricultural development. One factor was the heavy erosion of top soil, especially from hillside areas denuded of forest cover by the prevalent slash-and-burn methods of cultivation. In some areas the downward drainage of surface water produced under varied temperature conditions the laterization or the leaching of soils, which caused the surface disappearance of silica or of the clay and iron oxides needed as plant nutrients. Elsewhere excessive ground-water evaporation caused the growth of heavy grasses, which choked out all competing vegetation.

Hydraulic agricultural development contributed notably to the disciplined predominance of the leading peoples. These included the Vietnamese of the Red River valley, the Funanese and Khmer populations in the Mekong delta and the neighboring Great Lake region, the Mon, and later Thai, settlements in the lower Menam valley, and the Mon states of Thaton and Pegu at the mouths of the Irrawaddy and Sittang Rivers. The political importance of the central Burma area was based on the irrigated granary centers of Kyaukse, Minbu, and Shwebo. Subordinate centers of political and economic power developed in smaller arable regions along the lower shores of the Gulf of Siam, at Ch'aiya, Singora, Ligor, and Patani, which were also the termini of transisthmian portage routes for trade between India and China. The early predominance of Funan proper (Cambodia-Cochin China) and the importance of Champa derived from their strategic positions with respect to the coastal trade between northern Malayan portage cities and the ports of south China, as will be explained in a later connection.

The agricultural development of silt-rich river valleys and deltas called for sustained industry and advanced patterns of political and social integration, in contrast to the rudimentary political organization prevailing among hillside cultivators. Because the hill peoples were practically self-sufficient, producing little that was useful in trade apart from forest products, they constituted a meager source of profit except as slaves and were no political threat to the more advanced centers. As a consequence, the hillsmen were usually left to themselves.

Part of the resistance exhibited by hillside cultivators to assimilation by the economically and politically dominant elements of the population stemmed from the tenacity with which the former groups clung to their primitive way of life. This primitive way of life included traditional religious ceremonials associated with the selection of forest areas for annual clearing, propitiation of the spirits of mountain and jungle, plus planting and harvesting rites. Even if migrant groups waited until the expiration of the full term of years required for renewal of fertility of a given area before returning to it, the crop return was disappointingly meager. Sanitary deficiencies took a heavy toll of life from annual scourges of malaria and cholera. The debilitating problems experienced by hillside cultivators in terms of meager livelihood and health deficiencies also contributed to the general lack of interest exhibited by more advanced peoples in extending their governing responsibilities into the hills. Retarded neighbors were regarded as savages (*Kachin* in Burmese) or as a source of slaves (*Kha* in Laos). The continued presence of culturally backward peoples along watershed boundary areas affected historical developments only negatively by insulating the few important centers of political and economic power.

Leading Peoples: Mons and Khmers

The Mon-Khmer peoples, who moved into Indochina in B.C. times, were ethnically Mongoloid, but non-Chinese. Their languages are described as Austroasiatic to distinguish them from that of their Austronesian predecessors who also inhabited much of the Indochina peninsula. The Mons probably moved southward from western China via the Salween and Mekong River gorges into lower Burma and the Menam valley and the Malay isthmus during the first millennium B.C. and prior to their making contact with the north China civilization of Chou times (ending around 240 B.C.). The Mons may have preceded their Khmer cousins by several centuries. Burma's Mons were closely associated with the Pwo Karens, probably in a master-slave relationship. Their first capital was at Thaton, which developed in early A.D. times fruitful cultural and commercial contacts with India's Telengana section of the upper Deccan and with ports of the lower Coromandel coast. On the eastern side of the Salween-Menam divide the Mons established another state known as Dvaravati, with one center at Lopburi (Lavo) on the lower Menam and a second upstream around a capital known as Haripunjaya. For a time in the tenth and eleventh centuries a loosely structured Mon confederacy called Ramanyadesa included Thaton, Dvaravati, and Haripunjaya.

The Mons were widely dispersed and poorly integrated. They were seldom dominant politically, but were important both economically and culturally. Their substantial economic skills as hydraulic agriculturalists, craftsmen, shipbuilders, seamen, and traders were matched by their civilizing role as transmitters of Indian culture. Indian governmental practices and kingship symbols, Vishnu worship, Buddhism, and Sanskrit and Pali writing systems were all transmitted by the Mons to Burman neighbors, to Khmer cousins located to the east of the Menam valley, and finally to the later-entering Thai peoples.

The Khmer migration southward down the Mekong valley came to a halt short of the seacoast during the early centuries A.D. because it was blocked by the partly Malayo-Polynesian state of Funan. The latter was located in the delta of the great river and in the tributary lake basin of the Tonle Sap, which had apparently once been an arm of the sea until blocked off by Mekong sedimentation. As the leading political and commercial power of Southeast Asia from the second to the sixth century, Funan dominated all shores of the Gulf of Siam and also a part of Annam above the Mekong delta. The Funanese assimilated considerable numbers of inhabitants of the interior Khmer vassal state of Chenla before Funan fell apart near the end of the sixth century.

The Khmer conquerors of Funan proved incapable for some two centuries of reviving the older empire. Chenla was itself divided into Water and Land segments, and the stronger interior fragment had to cope with tribal rebellions developing in the upper Mekong valley. Lower (or Water) Chenla was divided for several centuries after 650 into a half-dozen petty states. The Chams along the Annam coast took advantage of the collapse of Funan to extend their control southward to the edge of the Mekong delta. The Dvaravati Mons also gained control over the mouth of the Menam River and down the peninsula extending southward into Malaya. Small but commercially important Indianized states, notably Tambralinga and Lankasuka appeared in northern Malaya. It was not until around 800 that a united Cambodia again emerged as the successor of Funan.

The Khmers learned much from the conquered Funanese, and also from the Mons, about the Indian symbols of divine kingship, Hinduism, and Buddhism. They eventually demonstrated in the Great Lake region their own superior talents in hydraulic agriculture, governmental organization, art, architecture, and literature. They occupied an area rich in food resources, both rice and fish, strategically located commercially with respect to the expanding China trade, subject to stimulating cultural contacts with India and also with the gifted Javanese, Chams, and Vietnamese. The China-originated Dong'son bronze culture (decorated drums and bronze utensils), which flourished among the Vietnamese and the Javanese, also had an important impact on Cambodia. The history of Cambodia after 800 will be surveyed later in this chapter.

To the east of the cordillera separating the Mekong valley and the northern half of coastal Annam lived the Vietnamese. They were a mixed race originating in south China, basically Austronesian but partly Mongoloid. They came to share some of the vocabulary of the Mon-Khmers and the tonal aspects of the widely dispersed Thai language. The Vietnamese were conquered by Han China around 111 B.C. and were subsequently fully assimilated as an integral part of China. They finally broke away from Chinese control in 939 A.D. following the collapse of the T'ang dynasty. Along with characteristic ceramic arts and silk culture, they absorbed during this millennium of Chinese rule the Confucianist ethical system, Chinese-type Buddhism, the mandarin bureaucratic tradition, and Taoist mysticism. They also developed into a highly disciplined and industrious people. The Vietnamese were involved in almost perpetual feuding with the Hinduized Chams occupying central Annam and in their only slightly less persistent rivalry with Khmer Cambodia. The Vietnamese thus played only a peripheral role in the affairs of the Mekong valley. They finally destroyed Champa in the fifteenth century and began thereafter a process of encroachment on the Mekong delta at the expense of the Khmers, a movement which has continued into the twentieth century.

Tibeto-Burmans

The Irrawaddy valley of Burma was occupied during the early centuries A.D. by a Tibeto-Burman people known as the Pyu. The Pyu capital of Śrikshetra (City of Splendor) was allegedly founded in 638, but the site was certainly occupied at an earlier date. The Pyu state apparently constituted the southern anchor for the Chinese overland trading route to India during the third and fourth centuries and maintained close commercial and cultural relations with India via the Bay of Bengal and the Arakan coastal region. For approximately one hundred fifty years after 638 the Pyu contested the control over lower Burma with the Mons, whose capital of Thaton lay to the east of the Irrawaddy delta.

The impressive ruins of Śrikshetra, including city walls, one gateway, and three enormous stupas, reflect an intimate acquaintance on the part of the Pyu with the Hindu cult of Vishnu in particular and with Indian Buddhism as well. The stupa ruins of the Pyu were copied from Indian patterns found in Orissa, while the many Buddha figures reflected Gupta and later Pala styles. A Chinese ambassador's report during the declining years of Śrikshetra described a walled and moated city, with a hundred monasteries devoted to training the youth of both sexes. The Pyu entertained an aversion, also present in Indian Buddhism of that day, to the wearing of silk cloth, because silk culture entailed taking the life of the worms. They also developed original musical and dancing forms. The Pyu were obliged to withdraw from the lower Irrawaddy valley during the course of the latter half of the eighth century to a temporary northern Burma capital of Halingyi (near modern Shwebo), which was later destroyed by hostile tribesmen from the Nan Chao state of Western Yunnan after 832. Captive Pyu soldiers were included in the armies of the inland state of Nan Chao on the occasion of its attack on Vietnamese Hanoi in 863.

The Pyu remnant remaining in the Irrawaddy valley was absorbed after 850 by a new wave of Tibeto-Burmans arriving in the vicinity of the irrigated Kyaukse area shortly after the collapse of Halingyi. The new group of Tibeto-Burmans apparently had proceeded rapidly southward into Burma's Shan states via areas of Western Yunnan normally controlled by Nan Chao. The invaders had learned methods of rice cultivation and terracing, animal husbandry, and the arts of war, but they had apparently sustained few, if any, cultural contacts with Chinese civilization. The Burmans gained firm control over the territory surrounding the three important granary areas of Kyaukse, Magwe-Minbu, and Shwebo. The Burman capital of Pagan was eventually founded on a bluff overlooking a bend of the Irrawaddy River a short distance below the confluence of the Chindwin tributary, and about halfway between Kyaukse and Minbu. Pagan Burma will be described in Chapter Three.

Thai Peoples

The Shan or Thai peoples, to whom several references have already been made, occupied at one time a vast range of mountain-valley territories extending along the southern China border from Yunnan and the two Kwang provinces, eastward to offshore Hainan Island. The most important of the several petty states of the region, ruled by a Lolo or Shan elite, was called Nan Chao by the Chinese. It centered in the region of Lake Tali, located just east of the Mekong gorge and standing astride the ancient trade route which ran from the Yangtze valley in the direction of Burma. Following the revival of Chinese power under the T'angs, in the early 600s, Nan Chao successfully resisted successive Chinese efforts at reconquest (attempted in 648, 751, and 754) and eventually allied with the T'ang to resist Tibetan incursions threatening both the upper Mekong and Yangtze valleys. One Nan Chao ruler conquered the Pyu capital of Halingyi in 832-35 and another invaded Tongking in 862-63. For some unexplained reason Nan Chao failed to prevent the southward migration of waves of Tibeto-Burmans into the Irrawaddy valley during the latter half of the ninth century. During the course of the history of Nan Chao, until its fall to the Mongols in 1253, separate bands of kindred Shan-Thais migrated southward to occupy the Shan states of eastern Burma, the upper reaches of the Menam basin, and the Lao country to the east of the Mekong. Lolo-Shan power in Yunnan suffered political decline long before its eventual liquidation by Kublai Khan's Mongol army in 1253.

The wholesale migration of Shan-Thai tribesmen into the upper Menam valley in the early decades of the 1200s resulted in the founding successively of Chiengrai, Sukhothai, and Chiengmai. Shan chiefs also played a prominent role in the liquidation of the Pagan Empire of Burma (1287-97) and in the subsequent repulse of Chinese invaders of Burma after 1300. Shan princes continued to exercise control over all of upper Burma until the rise of the Burman Toungoo dynasty in the middle third of the sixteenth century. Thai princedoms were also established at Luang Prabang and Vientiane in Laos, as will later be explained.

Ancient Trade Patterns

The meager extent of Chinese cultural influence on the peoples of Indochina (apart from the Vietnamese) can be explained in large measure on historical grounds. The center of ancient Chinese culture and political control was located in the Yellow River valley of northern China. The distant southern coasts extending as far south as the Annam littoral constituted by comparison a kind of half-barbaric backyard, imperfectly Sinicized. Neighboring peoples, by a kind of cultural osmosis, were welcome to learn civilization from China and thus slough off their barbarism, but such objectives were not the concern of the Chinese themselves. Confucianism itself in China proper fell under a cloud during the period from the Han decline to the rise of the T'ang (221-618), a period which witnessed the development of widespread Chinese interest in Indian Buddhism. A procession of Chinese Buddhist pilgrims found their way via the central Asian caravan route to the Ganges valley centers of Buddhist learning. No comparable Indian or Southeast Asian interest developed in Chinese institutions or religion, apart from the interest of the Vietnamese. Until well into the Sung times of the latter tenth century, when the magnetic compass came into general use and the quality and economic climate of Chinese shipping vastly improved, the preponderance of overseas trade at the south China ports was carried in non-Chinese vessels. Theretofore Chinese overseas traders participated, if at all, primarily as passengers on foreign ships.

India's interest in seaborne trade with China via Southeast Asia was, by contrast, of long standing, and it developed in a larger geographic context. It started around the beginning of the Christian era, when a lively demand for Oriental wares developed in the Roman and Hellenistic world of the Mediterranean Sea. Western traders, Greeks, Egyptians, Phoenicians, Arabs, and Persians traded actively with India's Malabar ports and with the entrepôt of Galle located in south Ceylon, but they rarely ventured farther east. This left to the commercial enterprise of Indian and Southeast Asian traders the development of traffic within the Bay of Bengal and northward via the South China Sea along the eastern shores of Indochina.

Near Eastern products for the Oriental markets, including frankincense and myrrh, medicinal drugs, glassware, fine textiles, and carpets, were never able to balance the payments due from the Roman world for imported Chinese silks and porcelains, for spices and forest products, such as benzoin, camphor, resins, and perfumed woods from Southeast Asia, plus ivory, exotic birds, sugar, rice, and ghee from India. The Emperor Vespasian in the 70s A.D. felt obliged to prohibit the further exportation of Roman gold to pay for such Asian goods. When Greek and Roman trade with India declined sharply during the course of the third and fourth centuries, the Sassanid Persians took over Near Eastern commercial operations, albeit at a reduced tempo. Around 500 came the permanent interruption of Indian trade in bullion from central Asia, which turned Indian attention increasingly toward the lower Malay peninsula as an alternative source of precious metal.

Under the active encouragement of the Indian port authorities, the trade in Southeast Asian and Chinese wares continued undiminished for several centuries. This contact set the stage for the Indianization process. Cultural sharing with Southeast Asia was strongest during the Gupta Empire (320-535), which constituted in some respects the all-time peak of Indian civilization. During this period and the subsequent Pallavan and Pala eras, centering in the

Deccan and Ganges regions respectively, India attracted admiration, both politically and culturally, from Chinese pilgrims and from the leadership of the states of Indochina. Southeast Asians found much in Indian art, religion, philosophy, and governmental institutions which they could appropriate with enthusiasm and profit. Therefore, during this time of disunity and cultural doldrums in China (between the Han and the T'ang), the Indianization process established a firm priority in Southeast Asia's cultural orientation.

The trade between the opposite shores of the Bay of Bengal followed a varied pattern in order to take advantage of the seasonal monsoon winds. These winds blew from southwest to northeast from late May to early October, and in the opposite direction from November through April. Bengali ships from north India utilized the winter season to proceed southward either to Ceylon or to the western shores of the Malayan isthmus and possibly down through the Malacca Straits. The isthmian portage routes were preferred by Indian traders prior to the seventh century because the Straits were pirate infested and the trade winds in the Straits highly uncertain. From the south Indian ports and Ceylon, the voyage to Southeast Asia could best be made during the summer monsoon. If the voyage were attempted at the very end of September, the ship might weather the storms of the seasonal change and then proceed down the Malacca Straits or along the western (outer) coast of Sumatra to the Sunda Straits separating Sumatra from Java. Either way, the all-sea voyage to China had to be interrupted at stopping points established at the southern entrances to the South China Sea to await the north-blowing winds of the fall and winter seasons.

Some half-dozen portage routes running across the Malayan isthmus were developed. The two most important ran between Trang and Takuapa on the Bay of Bengal shore to Ligor and Ch'aiya respectively, which were located on the lower shores of the Gulf of Siam. An alternative southern route connected Kedah and Patani, while another to the north ran eastward from Mergui. Two others from Moulmein and Tavoy ports on the Tenasserim coast proceeded via the three-pagoda pass and the narrow Meklong valley to Mon cities located in the lower Menam valley. Mon control extended at various times southward to Ch'aiya on the Bay of Bandon. Sumatran and Malayan traders operating from the eastern termini of the portage routes from the second to the sixth century functioned under the general supervision and naval control of the state centering in the Mekong delta known only by the Chinese name of Funan. Farther up the Annamite coast, the enterprising traders of Champa trafficked in legitimate forest products collected from the hinterland and also engaged in piratical activity.

Along the avenue of the major currents of trade with China, from the isthmian ports to Funan and on to Champa, the early pattern of Indianization was a mixture of Saivite worship and Buddhism. To the north and west of this main commercial stream, the enterprising Mons, with their capital at Thaton, located just east of Burma's Irrawaddy delta, became firm adherents of the Buddhist faith. Thaton maintained commercial and cultural connections with India and with kindred Mon peoples to the east in the lower and middle Menam basin. But whether Hindu or Buddhist in orientation, the courts of Southeast Asian states all followed the divine kingship pattern borrowed from India.

The Content of Indianization

Gupta India probably merited a claim to being the most orderly and civilized country in the world of its day. Buddhist missionary influence during the period spread southward to Ceylon, which eventually became the center of the Theravada faith. Indian ethical writings, political and legal treatises, codes of law (especially the Code of Manu), art forms, and epic Sanskrit poetry, all made lasting impressions in Southeast Asia wherever cultural contacts were maintained. In addition to the impact of the traders, some Indian historians have postulated as a prime cause of cultural diffusion an unusual exodus of talented people from India during Gupta and post-Gupta times, including craftsmen, artists, scholars, and Kshatriya (warrior) caste adventurers. Apparently no accurate way exists to measure the cultural impact resulting from any such migration, if indeed it did occur. But such considerations in any case cannot satisfactorily explain the full strength and character of the Indianization process. A major incentive certainly came from political leadership on the eastern Indochina side of the Bay.

The complex mosaic of Indian culture, with its multiple sects and philosophical systems and its ingrained caste stratification, could be adopted in Southeast Asia only on a very selective basis. The animistic peoples of Indochina, as the French historian Coedès pointed out, were receptive to the appeal of Hindu Saivite worship largely because it had developed in India by absorbing a large variety of spirit cults, including nature worship and fertility rites, cults which were similarly prominent on the other side of the Bay. The law of karma, found in both Hinduism and Buddhism, which affirms that deeds in one existence determine conditions of life in a later incarnation, also appealed to the Southeast Asians because it provided a means of rationalizing wide variations of fortune and status. However, the Indian caste system and the general subordination of womenkind, also characteristic of Hinduism, were unacceptable in Southeast Asia.

The most lasting impact of Indian culture upon Southeast Asia was the transmission of the Indian concept of the divine nature of kingship. The major Hindu gods, Śiva, Vishnu, and Indra, were allegedly capable of reappearing indefinitely in the persons of divine rulers, conceived as reincarnations of particular godly progenitors. The idealized kings of the Indian epics, such as Rama and Krishna, were conceived as reincarnations of Vishnu rather than Śiva, the destroyer god, who represented the principle of attrition. Vishnu embodied the positive principle of restoration as contrasted with Saivite attrition. A third major Indian god, Indra, developed from the traditional storm or sky god of the ancient Aryans of India, representing kingly power and authority. Indra was closely associated with the magical properties of the royal capital as well as with the person of the king himself. Indian cosmology posited the mythical abode of the gods on sacred Mount Meru, so that the actual capital of the "deified" earthly ruler was regarded as a mundane replica of Meru. The location was decided by certain cosmological and astronomical specifications for determining the center of the universe. The occupying ruler owed his divine status in part to the expert ministrations of Brahman priests at the court, and in part to his occupancy of the earthly Mount Meru.

Southeast Asian kings, by claiming divinity, enlisted the services of Brahman priests learned in Sanskrit lore and in magic to function officially at their courts. In Buddhist countries, as explained below, the kings were usually regarded as reincarnations of Vishnu or Indra, or they might pose as emergent Buddhas (*Bodhisattvas*) in their own right. Indian symbols of divine kingship, including royal regalia, the sacred sword and crown, and the white umbrella, survived in virtually all of the Indochinese courts down to modern times. Except for their responsibility as custodians of court rituals and symbolic properties, the court Brahmans usually played a negligible political role.

Indigenous to Cambodia in particular was the royal symbol of the nine-headed Naga snake, the traditional god of the soil and of fertility. The first mythical Indianized ruler of Funan, from whom all successors claimed descent, Kaundinya by name, was alleged to have married the beauteous daughter of the Naga ruler of the soil. The Naga serpent symbol was featured prominently in such classical monuments as Angkor Wat, and it is still found today as a motif in the architecture of leading universities of Bangkok. The association of royalty with the fertility principle, which was inherent in the Naga tradition, afforded a convenient basis for Cambodian accommodation to Śiva worship, under which the linga symbol became the very essence of royal power.

Other cultural borrowings included those taken from the literary treasures of India by Indochinese court officials and scholars. These borrowings included the principal Sanskrit treatises on kingship and governmental organization and procedures, plus the legal Code of Manu, historical epics and poetry, and Buddhist writings in the Pali language. Sanskrit and Pali also provided the bases for developing indigenous writing systems. Indian art forms, selected from numerous periods, found original expression in the work of Southeast Asian sculptors and architects. The best of the classical art represented a reinterpretation of Indian patterns; the worst reflected crude attempts at copying.

Variant Forms of Buddhism

The Buddhist (enlightened) faith, which became the religion of most of the leading peoples of Indochina after classical times, appeared originally in northern India during the sixth century B.C. as a variant of Hinduism. It protested the presumptions of Brahman priestly authority and the socially degrading implications of caste. The religion's acknowledged founder, Gautama Buddha, advanced a novel interpretation of life and destiny. He accepted several cardinal principles of Hinduism such as *karma* (the law of deeds), *maya* (the illusory character of physical existence), and *ahimsa* (nonviolence), but he then parted company with Hinduism. Buddhism offered a means of escape from the pain and suffering pervading all aspects of life. Man's involvement in an endless chain of suffering existences was attributed to his attachment to worldly desires and cravings, such as physical gratification, pleasures, and excitement. Emancipation from such cravings could only be achieved by following the eightfold path of right belief, aspiration, speech, action, livelihood, mental exertion, alertness, and emotional serenity. The latter attribute constituted the essential mark of enlightenment. The immutable Dharma, or firmament of the law, commanded that Buddha's followers: revere all forms of life, exercise truthfulness and generosity, take only what one was given, and avoid indulgence in drugs and alcohol. Brahman ritual and the caste system had no place in the Buddhist faith.

The social application of Buddhism involved contradictory emphases. At the mundane level, adherents were concerned with the performance of meritful deeds, which would afford them, under the doctrine of karma, the prospect of improvement of status and fortune throughout a series of successive rebirths. Such karmic morality was essentially relative and hedonistic, valuing socially responsible conduct as a means of lessening suffering and enhancing happiness personally. Buddhist aspiration at the nonmundane level sought the absolute goal of nirvana, involving the extinction of self and reunion with the all-pervasive essence of the universe. Such a goal demanded the repudiation of all earthly attachments, including the honoring of social and family obligations. Questers after nirvana became "pilgrims and strangers" in the world of men, repudiating social obligations along with carnal desire.

An attempt to bridge in some measure the chasm between the relative and the absolute objectives of Buddhism developed in north India during the Gupta-Pala period (350 to 600 A.D.) in the form of the Mahayana (Greater Vehicle) tradition. The prospective attainment of complete enlightenment was conceived as affording opportunity for the emergent Buddha to lend a helping hand in vicarious concern for less-favored folk along the way. This interpretation of the faith also gained wide acceptance in post-Han China. The less sophisticated Theravada version of Buddhism, which prevailed in Burma and Siam particularly, stressed the unique role of the historic Buddha, although conceding that several others may have preceded Gautama and that another would eventually follow. Theravada Buddhism put everybody on his own in the acquisition of merit via the dharma and the eightfold path and tended as a rule to regard pretentions to *Bodhisattva* status, especially on the part of kings, as akin to sacrilege. Thus the pretentions of Burma's King Bodawpaya, who aspired to Bodhisattva status by reason of lavish contributions to pagoda construction, were heavily discounted by those who cherished the monastic ideal of perfection. In post-Gupta India, the Mahayana sect virtually displaced the advocates of the Theravada faith, only itself to succumb in time to the embrace of a tolerant Hinduism. The island of Ceylon became the center of the Theravada sect after the 600s, and missions from Burma, Siam, and Cambodia journeyed to the island on repeated occasions to seek clarification and renewal of the standards of the faith. The Mahayana system gained temporary acceptance in both central Java (eighth century Borobudur) and in Cambodian Angkor (twelfth century Angkor Thom), but in the end only the Theravada form survived in the culturally Indianized areas of Southeast Asia.

Buddhist royal courts as well as Hinduized ones accepted Indian standards of divine kingship with little or no variations in practice. Theravada rulers were sometimes regarded as avatars of Vishnu, but seldom incarnations of Śiva. But Buddhism was strong socially where Hinduism was weak. Buddhism was generally oblivious to popular differences of status based on occupation or caste, and it could be propagated by missionary devotees including Southeast Asian converts and Indian pilgrims. No twice born Brahman priests or princely Kshatriyas were required for spreading the ethically centered and egalitarian faith of the Buddha. Buddhism was also a trader's religion. It, therefore, took on popular rootage. Hinduism, on the other hand, despite its assimilable quality in terms of indigenous spirit cults, was usually dependent for survival on royal favor and was, therefore, subject to the hazards of succession, economic decline, or governmental decay. Hinduism in Southeast Asia, except for the divine kingship principle and the pretentions to Chakravartin (Supreme Ruler) status, did not long survive the decline of direct cultural contacts with India. The latter began to fade in the twelfth and thirteenth centuries.

The Process of Indianization

Most students of Southeast Asian history are agreed that the principal initiative in the Indianizing process came from the Indochinese peoples themselves. There is no evidence of any attempted Indian conquest apart from the inconclusive Chola (Tamil) attacks on the Śrivijayan Empire around 1020. Adventurous Kshatriya military leaders may have been present in various areas of the isthmian portage routes and at Funan (witness the famous Kaundinya legend), but the Indianizing agents were predominantly literate Indian scholars or Brahman priests, perhaps including clever imposters doubling as astrologers or numerologists, who were invited to accept hereditary posts at Southeast Asian courts. Their functions were to contribute to princely authority and to assist in the development of centralized governmental agencies. The earliest Indian inscriptions in virtually every area, whether Hindu or Buddhist, were cast in impeccable Sanskrit, as attested by records of fourth century Kedah and Champa and of seventh century Śrivijaya. Outside the confines of the royal courts, the Brahman scholars played little part politically or socially. In the propagation of popular Buddhism, pilgrimages made by Southeast Asian scholars were so commonplace in post-Gupta times that regular hostelries were maintained in India for their accommodation.

Neither Hinduism nor Buddhism blotted out the indigenous patterns of popular spirit worship, which persisted alongside the imported faiths with apparently unimpaired vigor. In times of stress, traditional religious symbolism and behavior often displayed a kind of "activated inertia," and at all times the selective factors of local genius and preferences were operative. The Mons in particular demonstrated from the outset a preference for Buddhism, with a secondary interest in the Vishnu cult, as contrasted to their small regard for Siva worship. Funan and Champa, by comparison, were strongly Saivite in the early centuries, as was Khmer Chenla. The Thai arrived on the scene after the influence of Hinduism and Mahayana Buddhism had largely spent itself among Khmer neighbors, and little of it survived apart from the cult of the divine king. The persisting Buddhist cult in all countries of Theravada Southeast Asia came to terms with Brahman priestly roles at court and with older traditions of popular spirit propitiation.

Funan and Chenla

Before undertaking in Chapter Three the description of classical Indochina, what little is known of the history of Funan needs to be summarized. The early sources are almost exclusively Chinese, derived from reports of Imperial missions visiting the lower Mekong region in the mid-third century. The alleged founder of the prevailing dynasty, one Fan Shih-man, died around 225, while engaged in fighting along the western penisula borders. His usurping nephew-successor, Fan Chan (225-45), sought authentication of his title from the courts of both the Marunda King in Ganges India (240) and from China (243). This maneuver provided the setting for an eventual meeting of Marunda and Chinese missions at the court of the next Funan ruler, Fan Hsun, in 250. Subsequent Chinese descriptions of Funan, dating from 267 and 287, corroborate the early report. Closer ties between Funan and India and a corresponding recrudescence of Indianization developed after 357 under one King Chu Chant'an.

The dynastic title, Funan, meant "ruler of the mountain," and the prince was therefore "king of the mountain" in the Mount Meru tradition. The principal coastal port in Funan proper was Go Oc Eo, which was connected in the third century by some 120 miles of river passage with the inland walled capital of Vyadhapura (city of the hunters). The latter possessed buildings of brick covered with plaster and was located at the top of the Mekong delta near the hill of Ba Phnom at the confluence of the Tonle Sap River, which drained the Great Lake basin to the west. The strategic location of Funan proper, affording control of the sea lanes connecting the shores of the Gulf of Siam with the Annam littoral and south China ports, apparently contributed substantially to the state's wealth and political influence. The principal southern vassal states, Lankasuka (Patani) and Tambralinga (Ligor-Ch'aiya), which lay astride the leading portage routes, as well as Khmer Chenla located north of Funan proper, were ruled by subordinate hereditary kings. Only regions immediately adjacent to Funan proper were directly administered from Vyadhapura. Siva worship was well established under court patronage, and the Vishnu cult somewhat less so. Funan's five-century dominance over much of the Indochina peninsula left a persistent and prestigious memory.

Interior transportation within Funan proper was water-borne, using the Mekong delta, the Tonle Sap River, and interior canals. Products of Funan consisted mainly of rice, sugar cane, and cotton from the fertile plains of the interior Great Lake basin and fish from an annual harvest taken when the lake's waters receded. Extensive areas of the basin were irrigated. The people, including the frizzy-haired aborigines described by the Chinese lived along the waterways in bamboo houses resting on pilings. Cock and pig fighting were favorite pastimes. Taxes were paid in labor and also in pearls and perfumed woods useful in overseas trade; skilled craftsmen worked in gold and silver as well as wood, although stone ornaments and utensils were also in wide use. Indian influence, both commercial and cultural, was also much in evidence in the palisade-defended isthmian cities, and written communication in Sanskrit provided a kind of *lingua franca* for inter-regional communication.

The full impact of Gupta and Pallavan cultural influence, both Buddhist and Hindu, was reflected particularly in the celebrated reigns of Funan's Kaundinya II (died 434) and Jayavarman I (478-514). The characteristic suffix to the royal title, namely *varman*, was a Sanskrit term meaning "protégé of," which was commonly used by the princely Kshatriya caste in India.

Funan disintegrated during the last half of the sixth century when two Khmer brother princes of vassal Chenla seized control. The half-dozen Malay succession states along the isthmus assumed independent status, as did Mon Dvaravati (T'o-lo-po-ti to the Chinese). Chenla itself broke apart in the seventh century, with the ancient center of Funan proper dividing into a number of petty princedoms. Under Khmer control, Siva worship gained the ascendancy, but the Indianization process in Chenla slowed down. Meanwhile Guptan and Pallavan cultural impact along the isthmus continued unimpaired, even though commercial activity declined.

Around 800, a vigorous Khmer ruler, Jayavarman II, finally succeeded in reuniting the states of Water Chenla and in establishing Cambodian control over vassal domains located around the shores of the Gulf of Siam. The lower portion of the Annam coast above modern Saigon was taken over by this time by the Hinduized Chams. Meanwhile, the Buddhist Mon peoples established political and cultural ascendancy along both sides of the Tenasserim watershed and up the Menam valley. Mon Thaton became the teacher of the Pagan Burmans of the eleventh century, while Mon Dvaravati (from Lopburi southward to Ch'aiya) and Mon Haripunjaya (at Lamph'un) to the north became the mentors of the Khmers and later the Thai. Prince Uthong, a Thai leader long resident in Mon Dvaravati, subsequently founded the Thai capital of Ayuthia in 1350.

THREE

CLASSICAL CAMBODIA, BURMA, SIAM

The classical period of Indochinese history, from 800 to around 1350, witnessed the full development of two centers of cultural and political eminence, at Angkor and at Pagan, and the founding of a third at Ayuthia. Angkor was much the earliest of the three capitals, the site being selected at least fifty years before the Tibeto-Burmans appeared in the Irrawaddy valley around 850. Pagan emerged later as a center of power, in the middle of the eleventh century, partly as a response to Mon pleas for aid against the expanding Cambodian empire. Cambodian Angkor, however, outlasted Pagan. Angkor's domain was reduced to approximately the modern dimensions of Cambodia by the early 1300s, and finally succumbed to Siamese attack in 1431.

The political rise of the Shan, or Thai, peoples came in the thirteenth century. They aided in the final destruction of Pagan Burma, which had been started by Kublai Khan of China in 1287. The first Thai capital at Sukhotai dated from the early period of Mongol power, around 1220. A more pretentious Siamese capital was established farther down the Menam River at Ayuthia in 1350. While the Siamese state reflected much borrowing from the Khmers and the Mons, older Angkor and Pagan were, by comparison, more creative achievements. The latter two combined indigenous cultural and artistic resources with direct inspiration from Indian patterns, producing in both cases highly impressive results.

The Chenla Period in Cambodian History

As previously indicated (Chapter Two), the conquest by the Chenla Khmers of the lower reaches of the Mekong valley and the adjacent Great Lake area in the late sixth and early seventh centuries inaugurated an extended period of political decline. But the new Khmer elite were by no means barbarian. They had long been in contact with Indianized culture at Funan's capital city of Vyadhapura

47

and also with the Hinduized Chams, whose earlier domain the Khmers had actually occupied as their own Śresthapura headquarters (Champassak is still the modern name). The Khmers were acquainted with the Mons of the Menam valley, who had also penetrated the bordering Korat plateau.

The Chenla and Funan Courts were closely related. The Chenla prince who took over Funan, Bhavavarman by name (d. 600), was the son of a princess of the Funan line of Kaundinya, and he was himself married to a Funan princess. He allegedly seized control by challenging the spurious claims of a usurper son of a court concubine at Vyadhapura. The early Chenla rulers invariably claimed descent from the prestigious Funan line. They also retained the services of many of the hereditary functionaries of the Funan Court who were charged with both administrative and priestly responsibilities. The Khmers readily adopted the traditional Indian concept of the divine king and other aspects of Funan's religious and art forms. They tended, apparently, to follow the more strictly Saivite pattern of court ritual developed at Champa, originally a Khmer ally, rather than take up the moderate Buddhist trend apparent at Vyadhapura during the latter 500s.

Bhavavarman's conquest was completed by his successors, his brother and his nephew. His nephew, Isanavarman (611-31), established the first Khmer capital (Isanapura) to be located above the Great Lake. He also provided a daughter as the princess bride of the Cham ruler, so that one of Isanavarman's grandsons eventually became the ruler of Champa in 653. The Chenla Khmer victors were unable, however, to prevent the immediate defection of the former vassal states of Funan located around the western and southern shores of the Gulf of Siam, and it was several centuries thereafter before Funan's boundaries were fully restored.

Political troubles within Chenla proper and along its northern frontiers persisted for a number of generations and delayed efforts at reunification. Disputed succession claims and chronic rebellion in the Laos border country of the upper Mekong valley diverted Khmer attention from the less dangerous coastal area. The Chams took advantage of the confusion to occupy the coastline of Annam from Camranh Bay southward to the northern edge of the Mekong delta. The control of trade with China shifted temporarily to the Chams and to the rulers of a half-dozen city states, formerly vassals of Funan, situated along the isthmian portage routes. By the 680s, the center of seaborne commerce had gravitated to the emerging Śrivijayan Empire, centering at Palembang in lower Sumatra. Śrivijaya dominated for six centuries thereafter the growing volume of trade proceeding via the Malacca Straits, and it exercised during half of that period control over the southernmost portage routes of the isthmus as well. The several small Mekong delta states of Water Chenla (as opposed to the stronger Land Chenla of the interior) became more or less tributary to the rising Sailendra dynasty of Java during the late 700s. The last of the Water Chenla rulers was assassinated around 790, allegedly at the instigation of an offended Srivijayan king.

Early Cambodia

Near the end of the eighth century a returning Cambodian refugee prince named Jayavarman II, acting at first as a vassal of Java, undertook to unify the six minor political units which then made up lower Cambodia. By 819, when he completed the task, Jayavarman declared his independence of Java, and set himself up as a god-king in his own right. Brahman priests at court elevated the ruler to the status of a Chakravartin (Supreme Ruler) who allegedly constituted the living Saivite embodiment of the essence of kingship. Priests dedicated to the Naga-serpent tradition, indigenous to Cambodia, also bolstered his royal claims of control over the soil. By the time of his death around 850, Jayavarman II had established a feudal-type state by installing henchmen as vassal rulers of the several component areas. King Yasovarman I, by the early tenth century, ruled a domain extending from the Menam River on the west to Cochin China on the east, and from Chantaban on the Gulf of Siam northward into the trans-Mekong country. Land Chenla also became part of the Cambodian domain in the mid-tenth century, when the ruling Cambodian prince inherited both crowns. In time a fantastic concentration of catchment reservoirs, canal conduits, and irrigation works, plus a useful network of elevated roadways were developed in the heart of the kingdom, located in the basin of the Great Lake.

The role played by important priestly functionaries not only in executing ceremonial rituals but also in helping determine succession to the throne made the early Cambodian government something of a theocracy. Although efforts were made to designate a preferred heir-apparent, royal succession here as elsewhere in Southeast Asia presented unavoidable problems. The numerous sons of the five main Cambodian queens were all equally eligible for the throne, as were the younger brothers of the King. The prince who was finally selected by the Great Council of chief priests and ministers usually felt obliged as a security measure to eliminate most of his rivals and to maintain rigid restrictions on male access to the palace precincts through the use of Amazon guards. As occupier of a mundane Mount Meru, abode of the gods, one of the essential duties of the ruler was to act as the patron of religion and the guardian of the sacred law (*dharma*). Those members of the royal family who survived the customary purge, especially the sons of ranking queens, occupied a unique pre-eminence socially and were often entrusted with important civilian and military responsibilities.

Below the rank of the princes and the hereditary priestly chaplains of the Court came the royally appointed bureaucracy, numbering perhaps some 4,000 men. Chief Ministers supervised the provincial administration, military affairs, and the recruitment of forced *corvée* labor. They also had control over the police and the courts. All officials were required to take an exacting oath of loyalty to the King, which was frequently sealed by their contribution of eligible daughters for the royal harem. Judicial authority was exercised in the name of the King, but minor civil cases were locally arbitrated, and trial by ordeal was practiced when facts were in dispute. The palace precincts were inhabited largely by females. Below the rank of the five principal queens were the several-score royal concubines, who sometimes doubled as political hostages. Then came the professional musicians and dancers and thence down the scale to the servants and the Amazon guards. The usually overnumerous royal princesses, who were forbidden to marry commoners, were frequently used as diplomatic pawns and assigned to the harems of neighboring princes.

Classical Cambodia

The construction of architectural monuments at the capital city of the Khmers, Yasodharapura, began in the latter half of the 900s. The originators were Rajendravarman II, unifier of the two Chenlas, and his son Jayavarman V, who between them ruled from 944 to 1001. Early structures included the massive artificial mountain temple of Phnom Bakeng, located at the center of the capital, and the esthetically superior shrine of Bantasy Srei. After a decade of political confusion following the turn of the century and the accession of an isthmian Buddhist prince, called Suryavarman I (1011-50), the boundaries of Khmer control were greatly extended at the expense of Mon Dvaravati to the west of the Menam and southward into Malaya, following the pattern of ancient Funan.

Suryavarman's conquest of Dvaravati marked the breakup of the triple Mon Confederacy of Ramanyadesa; the two surviving members were Burma's Thaton and Haripunjaya, which was located on the upper reaches of the Menam River. Although himself a Buddhist and an enemy of the Saivite priestly clique at Yasodharapura, the new Cambodian ruler honored the Devaraja (divine king) cult and the traditional Hindu symbolism associated with it. He completed the five-towered Phimenakas palace structure and the vaulted Takeo temple, both of which foreshadowed in design the temple of Angkor Wat.

Classical Cambodia reached the peak of its political and cultural development a century later under Suryavarman II (1113-50), who was a great warrior, statesman, and builder. His reign witnessed the beginnings of the infiltration of Thai-Lao peoples along the northern borders, a development made apparent by the inclusion of Thai mercenary troops in the Cambodian army. Trouble with neighboring Champa forced the King to undertake three exhausting military campaigns during the period from 1123 to 1149. Suryavarman II extended Cambodia's system of hydraulic facilities, including reservoirs and irrigation canals, and completed an elaborate system of elevated roadways. His most celebrated cultural achievement was the erection of the magnificent Vishnu temple of Angkor Wat.

The heroic Cambodian efforts in warfare and construction of the second quarter of the eleventh century proved to be both costly and debilitating, so that signs of exhaustion were in evidence by the end of Suryavarman's rule. His successor faced a Mon rebellion and renewed trouble with the Chams. A Cham naval invasion actually destroyed Yasodharapura in 1177. Threatened disintegration was arrested by vigorous measures employed by the new ruler, King Jayavarman VII, who came to the throne in 1187. Allying himself with dissident Cham elements and employing Thai mercenary contingents, he was able to defeat the Cham fleet, to invade Cham country repeatedly, and finally in 1203 to install a puppet ruler. He also re-established Khmer control of rebellious Mon Lavo in the lower Menam valley. His domain was extended northward to the Lao-occupied territories around modern Vientiane at the curve of the Mekong and thence westward to include the older Mon principality of Haripunjaya in the upper Menam valley. His rule also reached far southward through the isthmus into Malaya proper. But the vast and fragile Empire of Jayavarman VII began to fall apart following the King's death in 1219. Champa regained its independence by 1223, by which time a new Thai principality of Sukhotai had appeared in the upper Menam valley.

Cambodia's decline, as previously suggested, was caused partly by the exhaustion of its resources of wealth and manpower in military ventures and in monument construction. The latter was connected with a new-found interest in Buddhism, represented in the Bayon temple at the center of Angkor Thom. Jayavarman VII's interest in Buddhist reform led him in 1190 to send one of his own princely sons to Ceylon in the company of a learned monk to study orthodox Buddhist practice. He also equipped the existing system of elevated roadways of Cambodia with resthouses at ten-mile intervals and provided a number of hospitals for care of the sick and infirm. These were progressive moves, but economic burdens were aggravated by the cost of maintaining an estimated 20,000 newly founded Buddhist shrines and several hundred thousand nonproductive monks and temple servants. Revenue deficits developed when territorial losses began. Seaborne trade with Sung China declined sharply after Kublai Khan's Mongol conquerers invaded south China in the 1260s. Even so, Cambodia proper proved better able to withstand the impact of rising Mongol and Thai power than did most of its Indochinese neighbors. Angkor's protected location and its highly developed agricultural base constituted important assets. A Chinese description of Angkor Thom as of 1225 portrayed it as a great center of commercial activity, where virtually every kind of product was obtainable. Chinese weights and measures were used in Cambodia's principal market centers, along with an indigenous counting system based on units of five. The city was destined to survive for more than two hundred years thereafter.

The most serious challenge to Angkor developed from the growth of Thai power in the upper Menam valley. At the fortified stronghold of Sukhotai, a Cambodian military commander of Thai ancestry assumed full autonomy following the death of Jayavarman VII in 1219. This rising Thai principality received shortly thereafter an important increment of refugee recruits from the faltering Shan or Lolo state of Nan Chao, which finally succumbed to Mongol-Chinese armies 1253. Sukhotai after 1275 found an able leader in Rama Khamheng (Rama the Brave), a younger son of the defecting Cambodian commander of 1219. The new ruler extended his conquests over important Mon sections of the old Cambodian Empire and over areas southward into the Malay peninsula.

Meanwhile, things were going badly at Angkor. The last important Cambodian ruler, Jayavarman VIII (1243-95), faced factional feuding at home and was, therefore, not able to mount effective resistance to Thai expansionism. Apparently, attempts to revive unpopular Siva worship turned Buddhist partisans against him. In any case, he was for a long time prisoner in his own palace and was finally assassinated in 1295 by a soldier son-in-law. Theravada Buddhism was clearly in the ascendancy by 1300. Angkor's position became strategically precarious after 1350, following the founding of the new Siamese capital at Ayuthia, located in the lower Menam valley. Nevertheless, more than eighty years elapsed before military pressure from Ayuthia forced the Cambodians in 1431 to shift their capital to the more defensible point of Lovek below the Great Lake. Cambodia's extensive hydraulic system of agriculture fell into decay, never to be revived. A little more than a century later, a series of Burmese attacks on Siam enabled the Cambodians to restore in part their ancient capital of Angkor, but only for a brief period from 1560 to 1590. Thereafter the Khmers declined to vassal status under one or both of the conquering Siamese and aggressive Vietnamese neighbors.

The Monuments of Angkor

The architectural achievements of the Khmers surpass that of their Indochinese neighbors in a number of particulars. The highly civilized Dvaravati Mons, by comparison, constructed no imposing buildings which have survived, and they never quite emancipated themselves from cultural standards borrowed originally from Gupta India. Champa's art forms were similarly India dominated. Its architecture was in brick rather than stone, affording opportunity for neither bas reliefs nor vaulted galleries. After cultural contacts with India began to wane, Cham art became crudely provincial, cold, and even grotesque. Stone construction permitted the Khmers to undertake bolder structural designs and afforded opportunity for elaborate bas reliefs. Over a period of some three centuries, the Khmers perfected the technique of stone construction, fitting pieces together in accordance with elaborate designs without the aid of mortar.

The most impressive of the Khmer architectural monuments was Angkor Wat, a Vishnu temple-mausoleum of the twelfth century. A rectangular site measuring 850 by 1,000 meters was enclosed by a moat and a colonnaded wall decorated in low relief on the interior surface. A broad elevated stone pavement some 450 meters long led to the temple area proper. It was flanked by a Naga-snake balustrade, with priests' quarters and a library building on alternate sides. The interior stages of the temple pyramid were enclosed by two concentric rectangular galleries. Lotus bud towers, nine in all, and originally gilded with gold leaf, decorated the corners of the inner gallery and the central mass, which reached an elevation at the center of more than 200 feet. The entire Vishnu legend, including the adventures of the heroic Rama and Krishna, was portrayed in the frieze relief carvings along the interior wall of the vaulted corridor surrounding the temple area proper. Also portrayed were many aspects of the life of the ordinary people. A monument of such vastness and intricacy reflected a considerable degree of economic and political vitality as well as the creative genius of the people who contributed to its construction.

A second impressive Khmer monument, the Bayon temple built by Jayavarman VII around 1200, was located at the center of his new capital of Angkor Thom. The city was square, approximately eight miles around, each side wall being bisected by a vaulted gateway approached by a causeway. The balustrades flanking the approaches consisted of giant figures of dwarfs supporting the naga serpent on their laps. A fifth gateway of similar character led directly into the palace area from near the northeast corner. On the three exposed faces of the towers anchoring the gateways, the impassive face of King Jayavarman himself, carved in high relief, looked outward in all directions. The motif was Mahayana Buddhist rather than Hindu, and the King was portrayed as an emergent Buddha, or *Bodhisattva*.

The Bayon monument itself was more concentrated in its design than Angkor Wat and the pattern is less easy to comprehend. The rectangular structure rose in irregular stages in a veritable forest of gilded towers, culminating in a central one of impressive dimensions. The four surfaces of each of the fifty-odd towers presented in relief the same facial image of the ruler-builder depicted on the five gateways. Wherever the observer looked, he encountered the haunting presence of the Bodhisattva King. The nearby royal palace of Angkor Thom was constructed of perishable timber, so that little of it has survived save the stone entry staircases and foundation façades.

The monuments of Angkor also show that despite the predominance of the Vishnu and Buddhist cults, important aspects of Śiva worship were also present, especially in the Devaraja (divine king) ceremonies, which were supervised by Brahman priestly families. The latter group also provided teachers for the royal princes, coronation officials, court physicians, and experts in cosmological architecture. The Brahmans can be identified in the relief carvings by their conical caps, their long hair, and their ceremonial gowns. Aside from their administration of the Hindu-type rites of the court, the sacerdotal families apparently exerted little political influence.

Monument inscriptions also help to establish that throughout the entire history of Cambodia, Sanskrit was treasured as a medium for literary expression and served as a kind of *lingua franca* for diplomatic communication. Standards of scholarship within the indigenous royal lineage were surprisingly high, as is demonstrated by stone inscriptions of creative Sanskrit poetry containing all the character-istic literary conventions.

Khmer Society

Cambodian society was highly aristocratic, even though hereditary rank was progressively reduced over five generations down to com-moner status unless renewed by the King. Mobility into the upper social levels was narrowly restricted. Commoners were liable both to labor duty and to military service. At the bottom of society were the slave elements, which included political offenders, war prisoners, and debtors. A characteristic aspect of Cambodian life was the prominent role accorded to Khmer women, not only in the local village and marketplace but also in Court circles and in the field of scholarship. Sumptuary laws specifying permissible types of clothing, housing, and accouterments according to rank were designed to prevent any-one from putting on airs. The vogue of Theravada Buddhism after the thirteenth century, however, may have operated somewhat to soften the rigidity of the traditional class structure.

The Founding of Pagan Burma

During the course of the first three hundred years of Tibeto-Burman occupancy of central Burma, from 850 to around 1150, the newcomers learned much from the older-resident Mon peoples of Lower Burma. The Burmans borrowed the Mon writing system, based on Sanskrit, and gradually assimilated Mon patterns of art, architec-ture, and religion. Burman power centered in three royally owned, irrigated granary areas: Kyaukse in the center; Magwe-Minbu to the south; and Shwebo in the north. Kyaukse had been developed largely by the Mons; the other two areas were developed later by the Burmans. Royal service personnel were customarily assigned to such choice lands. The capital city of Pagan was founded near the end of the ninth century on a bend of the Irrawaddy River between Kyaukse and Minbu.

For a century and a half following its founding, Pagan remained a relatively provincial center compared to the prosperous Mon com-mercial capital of Thaton in Lower Burma, which participated actively in seaborne trade and maintained direct cultural contacts with Buddhist centers in India. Only gradually did the Burmans of Pagan come to appreciate the value of trade and to replace their original barter unit consisting of a quantity of salt, with the Mon *tical* (one per cent of a viss of silver).

An adulterated Tantric form of Buddhism from neighboring

Manipur was practiced in early Pagan alongside a variety of indigenous spirit cults. The most important of the latter concerned the annual rites dedicated to the Sky God, who was supposed to inhabit nearby Mount Popa; another cult involved the worship of a pantheon of thirty-six vagrant *nat* spirits. Other forms of spirit propitiation, coupled with magic and astrology, insured the Burmans against illness, evil fortune, and harvest failure. Tatooing and the drinking of magical concoctions could allegedly induce invulnerability.

The political ascendancy of Burman Pagan over Mon Thaton dated from the accession of the illustrious King Aniruddha in 1044. Acting on the invitation of leaders of the rival Mon center of Pegu and against the wishes of King Makuta of Thaton, Pagan's military forces in 1057-59 aided in repelling invading Cambodian forces attacking via Tenasserim. At the conclusion of the campaigns, Pagan emerged as the dominant partner in the alliance with Pegu. The hostile Makuta and the elite of his Court, including scholars and priests together with a full set of the Theravada Buddhist scriptures were taken to Pagan as prizes of war. The victorious Aniruddha proceeded to transform himself into a universal god-king in accordance with the Vishnu cult. He and his Burman followers provided effective political and military leadership for the new empire. His Pegu allies and his Thaton captives contributed to scholarship and literacy, interpreted religious terminology and art patterns, and continued to conduct virtually all of the trading operations overseas.

Aniruddha's reign probably marked the first direct contact of the Burmans with the orthodox Theravada Buddhist faith of Ceylon. In response to appeals for aid from the hard-pressed Sinhalese ruler in 1060, Pagan sent military supplies to assist the island in expelling their long-time enemies, the Tamil Cholas of South India. The grateful Ceylon ruler responded by sending an alleged Buddha tooth relic to Aniruddha in compensation. The Mon scholar, Shin Arahan, was later sent from Burma to Ceylon in 1071 to re-establish in the island proper Buddhist ordination standards, which had been disrupted by nearly two generations of Chola conquest. The Buddha tooth prize was duly enshrined at Pagan in the new royal Shwezigon pagoda, alongside shrines for each of the thirty-seven *nat* spirits, the extra one being for the Buddha himself.

The Early Pagan Empire

Cultural leadership at Pagan was pretty largely monopolized by the Mons until 1113, the date of the death of King Thiluin Man.

This was caused in part by an arranged dynastic compromise designed to enlist support for Pagan from the heirs of the captured King Makuta of Thaton, and continued in spite of rebellion on the part of the Pegu faction following Aniruddha's death in 1077. The Burman military leader who took the reign name of Thiluin Man (Kyanzittha) on his accession in 1084, put down the Pegu rebellion and then designated as his successor the son of his daughter, who was wife of the heir of the Thaton line, thus bypassing his own eligible son. Mon cultural influence at Pagan Court in such fields as scholarship, religion, and art was unchallenged throughout the reign of Thiluin Man and continued strong under his successor. All royal correspondence of the period as well as inscriptions were couched in the Mon language and script. The ruler's closest adviser and friend was the Mon scholar Shin Arahan, previously mentioned as having been sent on the religious mission to Ceylon.

Thiluin Man's illustrious reign was noteworthy on a number of nonpolitical grounds. He planned and constructed the magnificent Ananda temple, which rivals Angkor Wat in the grandeur of its design and execution. He was also responsible for recording the Myazedi inscription (Burma's Rosetta Stone), which tells the story, in Mon, Pali, Pyu, and Burmese, of the King's deathbed reconciliation with the estranged son whom he had disinherited by his peace-producing compromise of 1084. Thiluin Man like Aniruddha exploited the god-king tradition to bolster his authority and was proclaimed an avatar of Vishnu following his death.

Buddhism and the monastic community played an important role in Pagan Burma. Religion provided the terrifying oaths administered in courts of law, while the monks served as teachers for youth at the elementary levels. The monastic community generally became the recipient of lavish gifts on the part of the merit-seeking wealthy, until Pagan's landscape was literally filled with thousands of pagodas and shrines. That religious enthusiasm reached the point of diminishing returns, governmentally speaking, is evident from the growing concern of the royal authorities with regulating monastic landholdings and curtailing new bequests. Entire villages, including people as well as lands, were assigned wholesale to religious institutions, thus robbing the King of personal services and revenue previously obtainable from such sources. The surviving records of pagoda gifts of slave communities provide, in fact, one of the best available pictures of Burman society at the time. Slavery in Burma seems to have been less onerous than in Cambodia, largely because of the practice of assigning entire villages to pagoda shrines.

The nonslave population of Pagan Burma was divided between royal service groups (called *ahmudan*), located mainly on the irrigated royal lands, and the commoners (called *athi*) living on family-owned lands. The royal service personnel were usually tatooed on the backs of their necks, markings which served as a means of identifying their superior status. The *athi* population, often of non-Burman origin, was subject to the control of royally authenticated, but hereditary, *myothugyi* headmen. The *athi* group was also subject to direct household taxes in addition to emergency services, military or otherwise, as the occasion demanded.

During the course of the long reign of Thiluin Man's grandson, Cansu I (Alaungsithu, 1113-67), a transition was made toward the development of distinctive Burmese standards of language and culture. The ruler gained an enviable reputation as a patron of Buddhism, the Burmese-type Thatpyinnu temple at Pagan, completed in 1144, being his greatest monument. Cansu I himself, as the great-grandson of the Mon ruler Makuta, preferred to use Mon and was trained in the Pali language, but Burmese cultural influence steadily increased. The later decades of his reign were punctuated by increasing political disaffection on the part of Burman partisans jealous of the Mon influence at Court. This was accompanied by the development of frontier disorders and by apparent friction over the commercial and diplomatic use of the isthmian portage routes.

The accession of the weak Intaw Syan, Cansu's son, in 1167 (or 1165), marked the beginning of a decade of confusion and disorder. The inter-regnum was ended following the restoration in 1174 of the direct Aniruddha line in the person of Cansu II, who brought to an abrupt end the Court's traditional deference to Mon traditions and language. Meanwhile, officially sponsored religious missions to Ceylon undertook to purify Burma's adulterated Buddhist standards of discipline and ordination. Cambodia's Jayavarman VII was another active participant in the effort at Buddhist revival in the late 1100s, as was previously indicated.

Patterns of Pagan Architecture

The twenty-square-mile area in and adjacent to the capital city of Pagan contains an enormous variety of pagoda ruins of all sizes and designs. Characteristic of the early Empire period and continuing active as a center of pilgrimage and worship was the Shwezigon pagoda, started by Aniruddha to house the Buddha tooth replica from Ceylon. It was a solid masonry structure, shaped like a step pyramid at its squared lower levels, which were transversed by four concentric passageways lined with niches for icons and connected by an exterior frontal staircase. The upper portions were circular rather than square, culminating in a bell-shaped spire capped by a be-jewelled umbrella *hti*. The corners of each of the square passageways were decorated by smaller pagoda spires, while much of the entire surface was gilded with gold leaf. To this same impressive but un-imaginative pattern of temple architecture of the eleventh century the Burmans were destined to return again in the thirteenth century.

The major architectural achievements of the two intervening centuries included a number of examples reflecting not only some fresh Indian influence but also the inherent genius of the Mons and the Burmans. The beautiful Ananda masterpiece of Thiluin Man was essentially Mon and Indian in its design and decorative detail. It multiplied by four and on a grand scale the typical Mon shrine consisting of a single darkened corridor leading to an encircled central masonry mass against which loomed an imposing Buddha image lighted from above by a hidden aperture. In the Ananda, the central piling was approachable from all four directions. The ground level was honeycombed by concentric passageways of varying ceiling heights, while many of the interior walls were elaborately decorated with terra cotta plaques and inscriptions. The highly ornamented roof portions were crowned by four lotus-shaped towers located over the several corners, flanking a huge central tower, all five of them covered with gold leaf.

The Ananda pattern was subsequently modified in the construction of two equally impressive Burmese-type temples, the Thatpinnyu and the Gawdawpawlin. The Thatpinnyu placed the Buddha images on an elevated platform at the center approached by interior stair-cases, which let in the air and light. The Gawdawpawlin was less elaborately designed, but was better proportioned and superior in much of its decorative detail. The earlier architectural designs were never completely abandoned, but by the thirteenth century, Burmese genius had apparently run its course, and building patterns reverted to the original pyramidal form illustrated in the Shwezigon. Pagan's extensive ruins constitute a largely unexplored museum of inscriptions as well as of art forms.

The Fall of Pagan

The early decades of the final century of the history of Pagan Burma witnessed the accomplishment of a number of qualified political gains. These included the establishment of more effective frontier controls to check Shan incursions across the borders of Nan

Chao to the north. Administrative innovations included the improvement of governmental agencies, involving a central Ministry, which combined both legal functions and the making of policy decisions. Governmental efforts to curb the excessive acquisition of lands by monastic establishments were only partly successful. In spite of these modest gains, lawlessness became widespread by 1235, and the government gradually lost its authority.

Serious trouble was encountered by Pagan authorities after 1271 from Kublai Khan's victorious armies from China. After defying successfully earlier Mongol demands for submission, a Burman army invading Yunnan met defeat in 1277. Border fortresses near Bhamo fell to the Mongol-Chinese in 1283, and the Irrawaddy valley was open to invasion. Faced by growing rebellion in Arakan and Lower Burma, the fearful ruler of Pagan decided to accept vassalage to China, only to suffer assassination at the hands of domestic enemies. The Mongols intervened directly by occupying Pagan in 1287 and by installing there a short time later a puppet ruler. Mongol influence declined sharply following Kublai's death in 1294. Chinese armies failed in two subsequent invasion efforts to consolidate their control over central Burma. Power eventually gravitated into the hands of three Shan brother chiefs, professional soldiers, who successfully defended the Kyaukse granary area against the final Chinese invasion in 1301. The youngest of the three brothers ruled until 1324, establishing a new capital at Sagaing across the river from the later Ava site.

Meanwhile in Mon-inhabited Lower Burma, a military adventurer named Wareru seized control during the 1280s, establishing a temporary capital at Martaban at the mouth of the Salween River. Although the new Mon state was nominally vassal to Siamese Sukhothai and far from unified at the outset, it eventually coalesced around Pegu as its capital and again became active in ocean-going trade. The Mons became famous in time as shipbuilders, marketing many of their craft at Muslim Malacca. Burman political hegemony would not be asserted again until the second quarter of the sixteenth century, this time centering in the provincial Sittang valley capital of Toungoo.

Characteristics of the Burma State

Several noteworthy variations from Cambodian and Siamese history are apparent in the traditions of Pagan Burma. In terms of religion, Śiva worship and Mahayana Buddhism, so prominent at Angkor, were almost entirely missing from Burma. One possible consequence was that the indigenous spirit cults of Burma were apparently somewhat less well integrated with the fresh Theravada Buddhist borrowing from Ceylon than was the case in older Saivite Cambodia. More basically important was the fact that Burman political power was centered far upcountry in the "parched lands" of the interior dry zone. Pagan Burma was dependent for major food supplies on the limited output of the artificially irrigated granary areas, or alternately on delta grain painfully transported up the Irrawaddy River. Burma's food resources, therefore, never approximated those of the intensively cultivated Great Lake Basin of Cambodia in its heyday, circumstances which resulted in a corresponding disparity in their respective populations. Possibly because the population of central Burma was sparse and widely distributed, the rulers of Pagan developed the practice of granting to royal brothers and other important personages fief holdings (*Myosas*) distant from the capital, from which support could be drawn. This tended to render politically innocuous the surfeit of royal princes who might escape the purgings which characterized changes of rulers.

Mon-inhabited Lower Burma was potentially as productive as Cambodia if delta lands could be developed along with water control systems, but such developments were inhibited under Pagan's rule. The Burmans subordinated economic expansion and foreign trade to political considerations and to their desire for the delivery at minimal cost of surplus rice up the river to central Burma. Inland Burma came in time to harbor a spirit of xenophobia and a disdain for outside commercial contacts, traditions which were entirely foreign to Siam and largely so for Cambodia. Burma also differed in that its population was ethnically far more diverse than was the case in Siam or Cambodia. Burmans, Mons, and Shans were sharply differentiated, not to mention three or four distinct Karen groups, plus the Kachins, Chins, and numerous other hill tribesmen. A final peculiarity of Burma was its vulnerability to overland invasion from China, a threat which developed on repeated occasions dating from Mongol times.

Siamese Hegemony after 1300

The situation politically in the Buddhist lands of Southeast Asia near the end of the thirteenth century found the new state of Siam without a serious rival. Cambodia had lost the entire Menam valley to Rama Khamheng of Sukhotai and to the smaller Mon state of Lopburi. Similarly the state of Tambralinga in northern Malaya had broken free from Cambodian control, while the rest of the isthmus and peninsula was falling to Siam. Leadership in central Burma lay with the Shan brother princes entrenched in the Kyaukse region and posing as the heroic defenders of Burma against the latest Chinese invasion efforts. The Burma-China border region, including the northern Shan plateau, was in a state of chronic disorder under a variety of Shan leaders, including the troublesome half-civilized Mohnyin clan. Pagan itself and the Burman city of Toungoo in the Sittang valley to the south became vassal to the new Shan dynasty with its capital at Sagaing, located across the river from modern Ava. Arakan province, located on the coastal border adjacent to Bengal, assumed its independence and developed a new dynasty of its own with its capital at Mrogaung.

Rama Khamheng of Sukhotai (1275-1317), who developed Siam as a major state, was both an able ruler and an astute diplomat. From the outset, King Rama Khanheng accepted without protest Peking's demand that he acknowledge the traditional vassalage relationship with China, and he thereby gained substantial moral support for his expansionist program. He adapted the Mon-Khmer writing system to the Thai language and made Theravada Buddhism the official religion of the state, although not to the exclusion of ancestral and nature spirits. His governmental system was fashioned according to Khmer standards, while his military recruitment and organizational procedures were based on Mongol practices.

Although suffering some loss of influence during the reigns of weak rulers following Rama Khamheng's death in 1317, Siam achieved cohesion after the founding of the more centrally located capital of Ayuthia in 1350 by King Ramadhipati. King Ramadhipati proclaimed a new law code, recovered control over Tenasserim, which had been temporarily reoccupied by the Mons, and captured the previous Mon capital of Martaban in Burma. He and his successors encountered chronic resistance from the former Siamese capital of Sukhotai, which had lost its leadership virtually by default in 1349. The Cambodians, as previously indicated, were obliged in 1431-32 to abandon their Angkor capital in favor of a more defensible site at Lovek below the Great Lake. Sukhotai's rebellion collapsed a few years later. Siam's hegemony was unchallenged for more than a century thereafter.

The greatest Siamese ruler of the fifteenth century was King Trailok (1448-88). He developed a centralized administrative system which included five functional departments, each entrusted to a ranking official. He also perfected a Code of Palace Law and implemented the useful practice of selecting a vice-king as heir-apparent to the throne. Diplomatically, the Ayuthia authorities continued to maintain vassal relations with China, even though the interests of the two did not coincide in connection with the establishment under Chinese sponsorship of the entrepôt of Malacca in the early 1400s. Siam claimed suzerainty over all of Malaya.

Around the middle of the sixteenth century, the Toungoo Burmans under able leadership and in cooperation with the dissident Shan border state of Chiengmai began a series of devastating attacks on Ayuthia, which will be described in the next chapter. The successful Burmese attacks so weakened Siam that the Cambodians were able to reoccupy Angkor after 1560 and actually to transfer their capital back to the old site in 1570. Both Angkor Wat and the Bayon shrines were restored. But the recovery was not destined to last. Following the death of Burma's great King, Bayinnaung, in 1580, the Siamese recovered their freedom and a decade later forced the Cambodians again to withdraw below the Great Lake.

The shift of Siam's capital to Ayuthia in 1350 had the unanticipated effect of encouraging the emergence in 1353 of the independent Laotian kingdom of Lan Ch'ang (the land of the million elephants). Taking advantage of the remoteness of Ayuthia and the weakening of nearby Sukhotai, King Fa Ngum asserted control over the Muong Swa (Luang Prabang) region and that of Vientiane, down river. The Laotians proper were ethnically akin to the Thai, sharing their language and their customs. Both peoples absorbed Theravada Buddhist religion and the indigenous Naga-snake cult from the older Khmer culture. Profiting from the temporary preoccupation of its neighbors (Vietnam was threatened by the Ming Chinese after 1368 and was interested in liquidating Champa, 1471; Ayuthia was involved in strife with both Angkor and Chiengmai), the new kingdom of Lan Ch'ang greatly expanded its control. Under Fa Ngum's son and successor, Sam Sene Thai (1373-1416), it dominated at one time an extensive area on both sides of the Mekong valley, including the entire Korat plateau.

Lan Ch'ang reached its peak during the 1540s when a Laotian prince was placed temporarily on the throne of Chiengmai, a city destined to become shortly thereafter a bone of contention between Burma and Siam. In 1547, the prized Emerald Buddha (Pra Keo) was transferred from Chiengmai to the new Laotian capital of Vientiane. Soon afterwards the original capital was renamed Luang Prabang, to honor the presence there of the venerated Golden Buddha (Pra Bang). The Laotian state declined sharply after 1571, however, when Burma's great King Bayinnaung captured Vientiane in connection with a military campaign against Siam. Burma maintained rather fitful control of Laos for more than a decade. The ponderous Burmese threat eventually forced the Siamese and Laotian governments to cooperate against the common danger.

When the crisis subsided in the late 1580s, Ayuthia promptly took over the dominant political role. The victorious Siamese not only drove the resurgent Khmers out of Angkor but also recaptured Chiengmai and established a nominal suzerainty over Vientiane as well. Following the death of the last great Laotian King, Souligna Vongsa, in 1694, a period of confusion ensued, which culminated after 1700 in the disintegration of the kingdom into four principal parts. Champassak in the south absorbed a portion of dwindling Cambodia and became an integral part of Siam, ruled by a local prince as Governor. Luang Prabang in the north survived as an independent kingdom under vassal relationship to Siam. The central Mekong riverine area centering at Vientiane occupied a status under an autonomous prince somewhere in between the other two, but after 1827 it also was directly incorporated into Siam. The interior principality of Xieng Khoung (Plain of Jars) shared the status of Vientiane until 1832, when it fell for a quarter-century under the suzerainty of Annam. Vietnamese influence steadily declined following the advent of the French threat along the coast in the late 1850s. Generally speaking, Siam's influence over Laotian peoples in modern times clearly predominated over that of their neighbors to the east of the cordillera, partly because of greater freedom of access between Siam and Laos and partly by reason of ethnic and cultural affinities.

FOUR

Buddhist Southeast Asia,

1530 to 1780

The history of Buddhist Southeast Asia during the 250 years after 1530 was a succession of violent swings of the political pendulum between the alternatives of Siamese hegemony and Burmese domination. The novel presence of the European traders, adventurers, and missionaries throughout the period was an incidental rather than a determinative historical factor as far as the Buddhist regions were concerned. Ayuthia was clearly in the ascendency in the early 1500s, having forced the Khmers to abandon their ancient capital site at Angkor in 1432 and facing no serious challenge from the surviving remnants of Burma's Pagan Empire. The picture changed abruptly after 1531 with the reunification of Burma under the new Toungoo dynasty and an extension of Burma's domain eastward into Siam and Laos. Ayuthia was twice captured by Burmese armies in the 1560s. Reacting to the collapse of Siam's power, the Khmers managed, as previously indicated, to return for several decades to their ancient center of Angkor.

The pendulum gradually swung the other way following the eventual decline of the overextended Toungoo empire in the 1580s and 1590s. New Siamese leadership emerged to drive out the Burmese, to re-establish control over Cambodia, and to occupy frontier areas bordering Burma. Siam seized the Tenasserim coast in 1615. After a troublesome bout with several European adventurers in the early 1600s, Mon Lower Burma was again subjected to inept Burman rule. Poor rulership at Ayuthia during the final decades of the century also paved the way for the decline of Siam and for an eventual revival of Burmese hegemony. The eighteenth century was almost a replay of the sixteenth. A new Konbaung dynasty reunified Burma after 1750 and then repeatedly invaded Siam. This time Ayuthia was completely destroyed (1767), but the invaders were unable to maintain their control for long. The Konbaung dominance came to an end with the emergence of the new Chakri dynasty, which operated from a new capital of Bangkok after 1781. This dynasty will be considered in detail in a subsequent chapter.

The role played by the Europeans during the course of these abrupt political gyrations revolved mainly around the activities of military adventurers. Portuguese gunners were enlisted in the sixteenth century armies of both Burma and Siam, either as mercenaries or as slave troops. Captives from French naval ships and from trading craft of the Ostend Company served similar roles in Konbaung Burma. Cambodian rulers in the late decades of the 1500s tried in vain to enlist European aid in support of their resistance to resurgent Siam. A coterie of Portuguese adventurers was later active along Burma's coast after 1600. The commercial presence of the Dutch after 1610 was, by comparison, superficially felt, and Dutch influence was concentrated for the most part at Ayuthia. A break between the Dutch Company and King Narai in the 1660s paved the way for the fantastic Phaulkon episode, which made a lasting impression on Siam's foreign outlook. During the first half of the eighteenth century, French and British agencies established rival shipbuilding stations in Lower Burma, where excellent teakwood was available. These holdings were eventually liquidated in the middle 1700s by the first Konbaung King, Alaungpaya.

Rise of Toungoo Burma, 1531-81

Siam had no apparent rival in Southeast Asia at the start of the sixteenth century. Burma was fragmented four ways. A disorderly northern frontier was overrun by half-civilized Mohnyin Shan tribesmen, who constantly harried the central area. Ava was ruled by the descendants of the Shan princes who gained control following the Mongol invasions. A Mon-ruled, prosperous Lower Burma state centering at Pegu was neighbor to the fledgling Burman outpost at Toungoo, located up the narrow Sittang valley one-third the distance to Ava. In contrast to fragmented Burma, Ayuthia's authority extended broadly throughout the Menam valley and eastward beyond the Mekong River. Cambodia was Siam's vassal as were many of the sultanates of the Malay peninsula. Siam's position in the peninsula was strengthened when the Portuguese captured Muslim Malacca in 1511, thereby fragmenting the once fairly extensive Malaccan domain. Siamese hegemony seemed very secure.

The rise of the Toungoo state took place with startling abruptness. The stronghold had constituted since 1300 little more than a safe haven for refugees from Shan prince misrule in central Burma, and its position between stronger neighbors both north and south was perennially precarious. An unexpected opportunity came after 1527, when the Mohnyin Shans captured and destroyed Ava, scattering its rulers and sending a new surge of refugees to Toungoo. An effective leader was found in King Tabinshweti (1531-51), who aroused his Burman followers to vigorous action. His forces moved northward to capture the central granary district at Kyaukse and then southward down the Irrawaddy valley by 1535. The Mon capital of Pegu fell to him in 1539, and Burman occupation of the Tenasserim coast strip followed in 1541. After defeating a Shan-led counterattack at Prome, in 1544, Tabinshweti was duly crowned as King of all Burma at the ancient capital of Pagan.

Then followed some forty years of intermittent Burmese warfare against Siam and Laos, to which brief references have already been made. Little progress was realized at first; Tabinshweti's initial attack of 1548-50 failed, and the humiliated ruler suffered assassination following his return to Burma. Five years of confusion ensued, threatening the disintegration of the domain. An able new ruler finally emerged in the person of Tabinshweti's brother-in-law, who took the reign name of Bayinnaung. He effectively subdued a Mon rebellion in the south, and then eliminated the remnants of Shan resistance to the north of Ava. When he resumed attacks on Siam and Laos, the Burmese forces were strengthened by Portuguese gunner mercenaries and by mounted Shan levies. Proceeding eastward across the Shan plateau, Bayinnaung's forces captured and occupied first Chiengmai in 1555 and then Laotian Vientiane. Bayinnaung later invaded Siam proper from both north and south. He twice captured Ayuthia (1564 and 1569), and he held it firmly until his death in 1581. Repeated rebellions in border Laos provinces consumed much of Toungoo Burma's energies throughout the 1570s in undertakings which proved to be as fruitless as they were exhausting. At the time of his death Bayinnaung was on the verge of undertaking the conquest of Burma's Arakan coast adjacent to Bengal. The extended Toungoo empire did not long survive the passing of its creator.

European visitors to Bayinnaung's capital at Pegu, rebuilt in 1569, were greatly impressed with its splendor and evidence of power. Imposing Buddhist monuments reflecting Bayinnaung's wealth and piety still survive in the vicinity of Pegu. On one occasion, he offered to purchase from the Portuguese for some 300,000 gold ducats a sacred Buddha tooth which they had acquired at Jaffna in Ceylon. Much of Pegu's pre-eminence was sacrificed during the course of the royal feud which normally characterized every shift of kingship. Bayinnaung's son, Nanda Bayin, attained a precarious ascendency in 1583, too late to stem the growing rebellion in Siam.

An important by-product of Bayinnaung's conquest of Siam was the opportunity which it afforded the rulers of Cambodia to re-establish temporary control over the traditional Khmer capital region of Angkor above the Great Lake. Portuguese missionary visitors to the area in the 1570s were impressed by the magnificence of the regilded towers of Angkor Wat. Moving northward and westward from Angkor, Cambodian armies invaded Siam's Korat plateau and even threatened to advance on Ayuthia. The recession of the Burmese tide in Siam following Bayinnaung's death in 1581 ended the dream of Cambodian recovery, for Ayuthia's pressure reached irresistible proportions after 1584. The harried Cambodian King Satha appealed frantically in 1588-89 via resident European adventurer friends, Diogo Veloso and Blas Ruiz, for military assistance from both Portuguese Malacca and Spanish Manila. It was all to no avail. Satha was obliged to shift his capital back to Lovek below the Great Lake in 1589, and that city itself fell to Siamese forces in 1593-94. A small Spanish-Philippines expeditionary force actually reached Cambodia in 1595-96, but the situation was beyond recovery.

Cambodia became thereafter for an indefinite period vassal to Siam and periodically a subordinate state to southward-expanding Vietnam as well. It eventually accepted French protection in the 1860s as a welcome escape from domination by its immediate neighbors. Cambodia's historical experiences go far to explain the near desperate efforts which Prince Norodom Sihanouk has employed to maintain Cambodia's independence since the withdrawal of French control in 1954.

The hero of Siam's recovery of independence from Burmese rule, Prince Naresuen, acceded to the throne of Ayuthia in 1590. He repelled successive Burmese invasion efforts in 1585, 1587, and again in 1592. After capturing Lovek in 1594, he occupied Burma's Tenasserim coast as far north as the mouth of the Salween River and then re-established Siam's suzerainty over the Laos country of the Mekong valley. King Naresuen staged an unsuccessful attack on the Burmese capital of Pegu in 1595, but the occasion supplied the impetus for the outbreak of disruptive Burman rebellions led by three royal brothers of King Nanda Bayin. Pegu actually fell in 1595 to a combined rebel force including an Arakan naval contingent aided by number of Portuguese adventurers. Siam's control of the Tenasserim coastal strip was fully established by 1615.

During the more than a decade of confusion in Lower Burma following 1599, two Portuguese leaders, Ribeiro de Souza and Philip de Brito, posing as defenders against the Burmans, set themselves up successively as rulers of a tiny Mon state centering at the ports of Syriam and Martaban. De Brito obtained some aid from Goa and managed to hold on precariously until 1613. The Portuguese garrison at Syriam was eventually captured, and surviving members, some 400 strong, were transported northward by King Anaukpetlun to the irrigated area of Shwebo to constitute thereafter an elite corps of musketry in the Burmese army. Burman rulers demonstrated no interest in overseas commerce and in 1635 moved their capital back to the more easily defensible area of Ava. They left Lower Burma in a condition of semidevastation. Ava's rulers became involved in a war with China over the Manchu succession in 1659-61, which was followed by a decline of dynastic vigor. Mon nationalism eventually reasserted itself around 1740.

Siam's Early Relations with the Europeans

The several successors of Siam's heroic King Naresuen (d. 1605), in contrast to his Burman contemporaries, actively encouraged overseas trade relations, both Asiatic and European. Newly arrived representatives of the Dutch and English Companies were both invited in 1608 and 1612 respectively to open trade with Siam. The English Company was unable to match Dutch competition and accordingly closed its Ayuthia factory in 1622. A particularly profitable Dutch outlet was found in Tokugawa Japan, which provided a ready market for Siamese hides, tin, and aromatic woods. Ayuthia received several hundred Christian refugees from Tokugawa Japan during the early decades of the 1600s. They provided personnel for an elite palace guard until 1632, when they became involved politically and were expelled from Siam. Although the Tokugawan Shogun in the 1630s moved to eliminate Japan's overseas trade entirely except for one Dutch visit per year to the Shogun-controlled port of Nagasaki, Dutch cargoes continued to include Siamese hides and tin. Dutch traders continued for an indefinite period to serve Siamese ports, although trade was interrupted for a time in the 1670s and 1680s.

Affairs in Siam began to deteriorate with the accession of an evil-intentioned usurper named Prasat T'ong (1630-56). The Dutch traders suffered arbitrary harassments which exhausted their patience. They were able to maintain their position only by flattering the unprincipled King, by providing lavish presents, and by according him occasional diplomatic and naval assistance at the rebellious ports of the upper Malay peninsula. That the authority of the Siamese Court remained largely unimpaired domestically despite the ensuing orgy of royal intrigue and violence was apparently attributable to the absence of exterior threat and to the continued potency of the traditional sanctions of kingly authority.

The accession of the youthful Prince Narai to the Siamese throne in 1657 was in many respects a great improvement, but it did nothing to facilitate Dutch relations. The impulsive prince developed in time a kind of phobia against the stubborn Dutch traders, who were apparently seeking a monopoly of Siamese trade. An abortive effort on the part of Narai to bring in English Company competitors in 1661 led eventually to a Dutch blockade in 1664. (This same year witnessed the Anglo-Dutch war in Europe which involved the Duke of York's capture of New Amsterdam.) The Dutch blockade helped them obtain a treaty recognizing their virtual monopoly position with respect to Siamese trade with China and Japan. Narai was diverted meanwhile by the opportunity afforded by the Manchu invasion of Burma, previously mentioned, to recapture border Chiengmai temporarily and to undertake an abortive invasion of Lower Burma. In a misguided attempt to develop a makeweight against Dutch predominance, King Narai invited to Ayuthia a motley group of exiles from Macassar (a port captured by the Dutch in 1667), who became in time extremely troublesome. Narai finally turned for assistance to French sources, which had established tentative missionary and commercial contacts with Ayuthia during the course of the 1660s.

Official French interest in Southeast Asia developed during the early years of the reign of Louis XIV at three levels, missionary, commercial, and political. French missionary interest stemmed in part from growing resentment at Paris against the presumptuous claims of Portuguese and Spanish authorities to an exclusive monopoly of Catholic religious patronage throughout Eastern Asia, dating from the Papal line of demarcation of the 1490s. Opponents argued that if success were ever to be realized, the active participation of the influential French church must supplement, if not replace, missionary agencies of the two faltering Iberian powers. The new Société des Missions Étrangères, organized at the University of Paris in the 1650s, was dedicated to the development of a French-trained indigenous ecclesiastical hierarchy. Prior to their departure for the Orient, volunteers studied at the Paris Seminary in a variety of Oriental languages and were commissioned by Rome as *vicars apostolic,* enjoying the titles of bishops of extinct sees.

The first two appointees of the Society, who departed for the Orient in 1658 en route to Vietnam and China, encountered difficulties both from the Portuguese and from the weather and ended up at Ayuthia in 1662, quite by accident. They encountered a surprisingly friendly reception from King Narai, concerned as he was at the time with finding a European counterweight to Dutch predominance. Relations were further improved following the arrival, during the course of the Dutch blockade in 1664, of the astute Monsigneur Pallu, head of the Paris Society. Pallu upon his return to Europe in 1665 expressed the definite expectation that Siam could become the center of French political power as well as missionary activity. After some delay, Pallu obtained both from Louis XIV's government and from Rome assurances of support. A Papal bull of 1669 established the jurisdiction of the French-sponsored church at Ayuthia over Catholic operations in Siam and neighboring states. Meanwhile, in 1664, the French East India Company had been revived under royal patronage.

The establishment of political contact between the French government and that of Siam was delayed for a number of reasons. The French fleet sent to the Bay of Bengal in 1668 became involved in an unsuccessful collaboration with the anti-Dutch ruler of Kandy in Ceylon in an effort to expel Dutch influence from the island. The French admiral eventually established the French post at Pondicherry, India, in 1672. Near the end of the ensuing Franco-Dutch war in Europe (1672-78), a French ship en route to Siam was captured by the Dutch. Two years later, a Siamese ship on the way to France wrecked off Madagascar Island. A French Company agent first visited Ayuthia in 1680, and it was 1682 before a French-led mission from Siam actually reached Paris.

Meanwhile, in 1678, a coterie of ex-employees of the English Company reached the Siamese capital where English factory assets were being liquidated. They included George Barnaby, Samuel White, and a precocious Greek linguist named Constantine Phaulkon. The Greek mastered the Siamese language within two years and subsequently obtained appointment by King Narai as interpreter and eventually as Superintendent of Foreign Trade. He thus became a key person in the conduct of negotiations with foreign visitors. Phaulkon placed friends Barnaby and White in charge of the isthmian port of Mergui in 1685-86, whence they began to prey on Indian shipping in the Bay of Bengal. It was with Phaulkon that French Company representatives and Jesuit representatives of the Court of Louis XIV came to deal after 1682. Phaulkon became a confidant of Jesuit spokesmen and a convert to the Catholic faith.

Serious negotiations between Phaulkon and the French Jesuit Father Tachard led to the dispatch of a second French-led Siamese mission to Europe in 1684. The French mission which arrived at Ayuthia in the following year achieved, with Phaulkon's help, the conclusion of a treaty granting commercial concessions to the French Company and rights of missionary access. In return the French by implication agreed to send out a military force to garrison the Malay port of Singora, threatened at the time by Dutch naval action. An unofficial agreement between Phaulkon and Father Tachard at the time also proposed the recruitment in France of several-score able French administrators whom Phaulkon would later assign to strategic posts in the Siamese government. When the proposed treaty accord reached Paris, Louis XIV's Ministers decided to augment their demands to include full extraterritorial rights for resident Frenchmen, and the assignment of French garrisons to both Mergui and Bangkok. An imposing force of six French warships and more than 600 soldiers was dispatched to Siam in 1687.

The Tachard-Phaulkon conspiracy failed for several reasons. A sizable fraction of the French force died from illness during the course of the ocean voyage, and a number of others were incapacitated upon their arrival. Before any garrison assignments were made, the entire force had to take an oath of allegiance to King Narai. Some 200 troops were eventually stationed at Bangkok, 120 at Mergui, with fewer than one hundred others scattered variously. Treaty revisions demanded by the French covering control over offshore islands within a ten-mile radius of Mergui plus full extraterritorial rights confirmed the suspicions of Phaulkon's enemies at the Court. His position became completely untenable in the spring of 1688 when Narai became seriously ill. Phaulkon was accordingly arrested in May and executed in June 1688; Narai himself died in July. In the end, both the Missions Étrangères and the French garrison had deserted the wily Greek. French soldiers were subsequently evacuated from Mergui to Pondicherry in Siamese ships.

King Narai's dangerous flirtation with foreign adventurers produced long-term effects on the history of Siam. European foreigners for many generations thereafter were understandably suspect, and more than 150 years would pass before the Siamese authorities would again welcome foreign contacts. The Dutch resumed their trading at Ayuthia in a desultory way, and representatives of the Paris missionary society continued their rather ineffectual activities. More important was the discredit which the monarchy itself suffered as a result of foreign intrigues. Following Narai's death, the crown was seized by an uncouth and vengeful soldier named P'etraja, who ruled until 1701. Thereafter, successions to the throne were marred by palace coups and occasionally by protracted military strife, situations which aggravated the growing demoralization of both the royal Court and the army. Along both shores of Siamese Malaya, piracy and kidnapping became endemic. Siamese political hegemony had run its course by the middle 1700s, when Ayuthia was again obliged to face the explosive might of a reunified Burma.

The Rise of Burma's Konbaung Dynasty

The history of the kingdom of Burma for a century following the withdrawal of its capital to inland Ava in 1635 was one of fairly steady decline. Something was accomplished, however, during the middle 1600s in the improvement of law codes, in the preparation of a landholding inventory, and in coordination of the central administrative agencies under the central Hlutdaw Council. Otherwise gains were minimal. Ava's unavoidable involvement in the border feudings of China's Ming and Manchu partisans after 1658 was a contributing factor. Successive rulers were weak and their reigns were shortlived, with successions marred by vengeful palace coups. Manipuri raiders occupied the Kabaw River valley, western tributary to the Chindwin River, and initiated a series of destructive incursions into the heart of the central Irrawaddy valley. The Mon-inhabited areas of Lower Burma suffered meanwhile from oppressive misrule and from Burman neglect of the region's commercial possibilities. An alien factor was introduced in the early 1700s when British and French rivals in the Bay of Bengal established successively naval repair stations at the delta port of Syriam for use during the winter monsoon season. Both European companies invariably encountered a discouraging response to their efforts to develop profitable trade relations with Burma.

The power of the Ava government reached an all-time nadir after 1740. Manipuri raiders threatened the capital from the outside, while within the city the Court was embarrassed by a rebellion involving Mon and Shan prisoners. At this juncture, Mon rebels in Lower Burma eliminated the Burman Governor (*Myo-wun*) at Pegu, seized the seaports of the delta, and extended their control upriver to Prome, which they captured in 1743. Harried by its problems nearer home, Ava was able to make no effective rejoinder. The Mons eventually found even more competent leadership around 1747 in the person of the ambitious King Binnya Dala and were able to resume their conquest. They captured Ava in 1752, and the Burman cause appeared lost. But the Mons misjudged the virulence of the Burman reaction when they left too small a garrison at Ava. The apparent disaster was actually the signal for a third historic demonstration of the explosive energies of Burmese national spirit under the leadership of the Konbaung dynasty.

The new Burman leader was the son of a township headman at the granary center of Shwebo, located north of Ava and across the river. He assumed the pretentious name of Alaungpaya (Embryo Buddha). Rallying his power at Shwebo, he forced the feeble Mon garrison to withdraw from Ava in 1753 and then proceeded to consolidate his authority throughout Upper Burma. Taking advantage of dissension among his Mon enemies, he extended his control into Lower Burma by 1756. The French garrison at Syriam made the mistake of allying with the Mons and was captured, along with quantities of military supplies. The Burmans acquired two-score French cannon, some 1,300 muskets, and two hundred fighting men, who were added to the Burman army. The Mon capital of Pegu fell to Alaungpaya in the following year. Tardiness on the part of the British Company in evacuating its post of Negrais on the western corner of the delta exposed its caretaker staff to Burman massacre in 1759. European prestige was understandably low. The belligerence of Alaungpaya's victorious army was then directed toward Siam, whither many of the Mon refugees from Pegu and its environs had fled.

The enfeebled Siamese government proved incapable in the end of stemming the spirited Burmese invasion. Ayuthia was successfully defended in 1760 only because King Alaungpaya was injured by a badly handled siege gun and died on his way back to Burma. The problem of arranging the succession caused considerable delay, so that it was 1764 before one of his sons, Hsinbyushin, was installed as king at the now restored capital of Ava. Attacks on Ayuthia were renewed in 1766, and the city fell to King Hsinbyushin after a siege lasting more than a year. This time Ayuthia was utterly destroyed, a wanton act which the Siamese will ever remember. Immediately thereafter, however, the Burmese armies had to return home to repel a series of Chinese incursions from Yunnan, which may or may not have been connected with Burma's preoccupations in the Menam valley. The Chinese forces were repulsed with some difficulty, and Burma was obliged to agree to resume the sending of periodic tribute missions to Peking. A subsequent Mon rebellion in Lower Burma which persisted until 1773 afforded the Siamese additional time to reorganize their defenses. King Singu, Alaungpaya's weakling grandson who acceded to the throne in 1776, was obliged to abandon for a time the effort to reconquer Siam.

In the absence of qualified and capable leadership, Siam's recovery was slow. The first successful leader of the opposition to renewed Burmese invasions was a half-Chinese provincial official named P'ya Taksin, who took over temporarily as king. He was eventually displaced at the new capital site of Bangkok in 1782, by the founder of the Chakri dynasty, itself partly Chinese in ancestry. Meanwhile a new and more vigorous king had come to power in Ava, Bodawpaya (1782-1819), uncle of Singu and one of the abler of Alaungpaya's sons. His first concerns were to found a new capital at Amarapura, some six miles north of Ava, to conquer the Arakan kingdom in 1784, and to occupy the Tenasserim coast which had been controlled by the Siamese since 1615. He then turned his attention in 1785 to the reconquest of Siam. In spite of Bodawpaya's acknowledged ability, he demonstrated little common sense as to what was feasible and necessary to undertake. Over a period of seventeen years, from 1785 to 1802, he squandered Burma's energies and resources in five abortive efforts to dominate Siam. The net result territorially was to lose to Bangkok Burma's former vassal city of Chiengmai. These efforts were punctuated in the 1790s by repressive actions against the Mons, Karens, and Arakanese of Lower Burma, who rebelled repeatedly against the heavy exactions levied upon them by royal officials.

Foiled in realizing his military ambitions in Siam, the prideful Bodawpaya sought to re-establish his damaged prestige by other means. To the distress of leading members of the orthodox Buddhist hierarchy, he laid claim to the exalted status of a *Bodhisattva* (Emergent Buddha). He undertook to buttress his position as a patron of Buddhism by attempting the construction of a fabulously huge pagoda structure at Mingun, across the river from Amarapura. Involvement in this burdensome obsession was accompanied by the King's neglect of governing responsibilities, and this led to the development of widespread lawlessness and the consequent impoverishment of most of Upper Burma. Bodawpaya's contemporaneous imposition of arbitrary military control over the hitherto autonomous Shan princes of the eastern plateau region contributed to their loss of both prosperity and dignity and also eroded away any semblance of loyalty on the part of the Shans to the Konbaung regime. By the end of Bodawpaya's long reign in 1819, Burma's power was clearly in decline, and its government had developed a frontier quarrel with

British rule in neighboring Bengal, to which attention must now be turned.

Burmese Relations with British Bengal, 1784-1826

Friction between Burmese Arakan and British Chittagong coastal areas developed in the 1790s as a result of the flight of Arakan refugees, both rebel and nonpolitical, across the ill-policed boundary. British authorities in Bengal at the time were too concerned with preventing their French enemies from establishing a naval foothold on the lower Burma coast to risk imperilling relations with Bodawpaya's government. They agreed, therefore, to repatriate rebel refugees and to close the Chittagong border to further entry. Relations remained thereafter reasonably friendly until 1811, when an Arakanese rebel leader operating from a base in Chittagong invaded Arakan and captured the provincial capital of Mrogaung. Burman forces recovered control and chased rebel elements back across the boundary. Bengal authorities challenged the intrusion and refused to turn over to Burma rebel elements held in British custody. Relations improved temporarily after the death of the Arakan leader in 1815, but shortly thereafter the problem of border relations took on a new dimension. Agents of Amarapura began to exert pressure on the interior Indian border states of Manipur, Chahar, and Assam to install puppet princes. The two imperialisms were destined to clash in 1824-25.

The accession of Burma's ambitious King Bagyidaw in 1819, upon the death of his father, stimulated Amarapura's aggressive designs against British Bengal. The Burmans had some reasons for confidence. Their spirited army had an able leader in General Bandoola. The border states of India were virtually defenseless, and Burma itself had never suffered massive invasion from the Indian side. Burmans also remembered that they had repelled repeated Chinese invasions, succumbing only to that of the Mongols. What Burmese expansionists did not take into account was the extent to which the British-Indian authorities since 1760 had succeeded in mobilizing the resources and manpower of the subcontinent or the importance of British domination of the sea lanes of the Bay of Bengal. Following the collapse of the Dutch commercial empire in the 1790s, the ships of the English Company and privately owned "country vessels" licensed by it had taken over most of the India-China trade. By 1820, the British were in control of Penang Island (1786), neighboring Province Wellesley (1800), Malacca (1795), Ceylon (1815), and Singapore Island (1819). The British-led Sepoy troops were well trained and well equipped, and they could be transported to any port in the Bay of Bengal and effectively supported by sea for an indefinite period of time.

General Bandoola's ambitious attempt to invade Bengal via Manipur and Assam during the late spring of 1824 was cut short abruptly by the surprise landing of a British-Indian expeditionary force at Rangoon. Although the European-led invaders were unable to proceed inland during the ensuing rainy season and suffered heavy losses from illness, they managed to withstand a prolonged siege of Rangoon in the autumn of 1824 until re-enforcements could arrive. The besieging army was eventually driven off and defeated. General Bandoola was himself killed in April 1825. But again it was too late in the dry season to advance northward before the monsoon rains began. The final British-Indian push came in the fall of 1825, aided by an armed steamer operating on the Irrawaddy. Mon and Karen rebellions had developed meanwhile in the Irrawaddy delta areas.

British victory and the resulting treaty of Yandabo of 1826 inflicted a deep humiliation on the Burman Court. Burma's material losses were substantial, including the cession of both the Arakan and Tenasserim coastal regions and the payment of a one-million-pound indemnity. Possibly even more serious was the irreparable loss of face inflicted on the proud Konbaung dynasty. It had been defeated in its attempt to invade Bengal and now was explicitly forbidden by treaty to attack its traditional enemy, Siam. To other material losses were added the devastating punishment inflicted subsequently by Burman armies on the overextended Mon and Karen rebels in the south, who had expected British support, plus the cost of building a new capital city at the Ava site to replace ill-omened Amarapura. Burma's proximity to British India and the transformation of the Bay of Bengal into a British lake made relations with India thereafter a matter of overriding concern to the Burmese authorities. King Bagyidaw became moody and ineffective and eventually went insane. The same affliction overtook his unscrupulous brother and successor, Prince Tharawaddy, who took over in 1838.

FIVE

PARTING OF THE WAYS:

MINDON AND MONGKUT

Despite the recurring antagonisms characterizing historically the relations between Burma, Siam, Cambodia, and Laos, the
respective governmental and social institutions and the cultural and
religious values of the four countries remained very similar. Few
descriptive generalizations could be advanced concerning one of them
which were not equally applicable to the other three. Their sources
of cultural development were very much the same, and the circumstances of their historical evolution were comparable. The Burmans
had borrowed much from their Mon neighbors, and had in turn contributed their own writing system and religion to the minor Shan
states of the eastern plateau. The later arriving Siamese had ap-
propriated patterns of the older Mon and Khmer civilizations, while
the culture of the Laotian occupants of the Mekong valley lowlands
was simply a provincial projection of that of their Siamese kinsmen.
The divine king pattern of princely authority and the Theravada
Buddhist system of religion were standard everywhere.

The nineteenth century marked a substantial parting of the ways
culturally among the Theravada Buddhist people of Southeast Asia.
Burma fell by stages under the domination of British India and was
threatened with loss of its cultural as well as its political identity. An
alien legal and administrative system was imposed, while outside contacts educationally and economically were channeled in the direction
of India and Great Britain. During a near century of relatively stable
administration, Indian labor and British and Indian capital inaugurated an intensive development of Burma's agricultural, forestry,
and mineral resources, but at heavy cost in terms of social and political vitality. By contrast, Cambodia and Laos fell under the protection of French colonial authorities, who superimposed on the
elite classes a mild veneer of Gallicization. The French interfered
little with educational, economic, political, and social patterns traditional to the Khmer and Lao peoples, while capitalizing on the

78

desire of both groups to escape from vassalage to Siam. The able Chakri dynasty of Bangkok, by further contrast, managed in the nick of time to reach diplomatic and commercial accommodation with the dominant Western interests and thus maintained Siam's political and cultural integrity. Bangkok was obliged to surrender to the French substantial territorial claims in Cambodia and the Mekong valley and to the British much of Malaya, but the essential core of Siamese territory was kept intact. These varied experiences of the several countries with Western colonialism fashioned divergent tendencies which affected their later histories. This chapter will compare the mid-nineteenth century policies and experiences of Burma and Siam in dealing with the rising impact of the West.

Similarities and Differences between Burma and Siam

The principal similarities in political institutions prevailing between Burma and Siam, as previously indicated, stemmed from their common acceptance of the Indian pattern of divine kingship. Magically expert Brahman priests at both Courts supervised the coronation rituals, guaranteed the authenticity of the royal regalia, selected auspicious dates and capital sites, and were much in evidence at all formal Court ceremonies. The authority of kingship involved the legal ownership of all lands within the state's domain, as well as plenary claims on the persons and services of all subjects. Government officials from the highest levels downward were, under the law, "slaves" of the monarch, and all of them exercised power in the name of the ruler and at his pleasure. Buddhism in both countries was highly revered, but kings were careful to keep the influential monastic community under strict royal control and to deny the monks any political role. Rulers enhanced their prestige by lavish patronage of the Buddhist faith.

Governmental administrative institutions in the two countries were also very similar. Burma's highest *Hlutdaw* Council was the counterpart of the *Senabodi* at Bangkok. Control of foreign relations in both countries was entrusted in large measure to the hands of officials posted on the frontiers. These included the Governors (*Myowuns*) at Rangoon and on the China border at Bhamo for Burma, and the Ministers of the North and South (Burma and Malaya respectively) in Siam. Subordinate princes in both realms were assigned income from land revenues for their personal maintenance. Local government in both countries was under the control of the township headmen, a locally selected patron in Siam and a hereditary *myothugyi* in Burma. In both countries the higher provincial officials were centrally appointed. Theravada Buddhism was so closely identified with the character of the two states that the majority peoples in both countries were virtually impervious to the appeals of resident Christian missionaries. Both governments down to the 1850s were wary if not openly hostile to the assumed machinations of the Europeans, and both maintained a nominal vassal relationship with China.

Several points of divergence between Burma and Siam were significant. The Siamese state had borrowed from the Cambodians a number of traditions which were foreign to Burma. These included the principle of the erosion of social status in successive generations down the five grades of princely rank. The Naga snake's reputation as lord of the soil and the waters had no comparable equivalent in Burma. The Buddhist tradition in Siam also reflected a distinctive suggestion of Khmer Mahayana influence in the borrowing of merit by participants in ritual occasions, such as the entry of a youth into the monastic order. Chinese cultural patterns were also notably present among the Siamese while relatively absent among the Burmese. Methods for pacifying malevolent spirits and determining auspicious days, significant language similarities, and the operation of a modified mandarinate system in Siam all reflected a closer affinity with China than could be found in Burma. Siamese tradition also put greater emphasis on filial and kinship relationships. Siam's population was considerably more homogenous than that of Burma, where the Mons and the Karens of the delta and central valleys remained alien to the majority Burman group. The mountainous periphery of Burma included alien Chin, Kachin, and Shan peoples, plus scores of minor tribal groupings. Temperamentally, the Burmans appeared more explosively volatile than their Siamese neighbors, especially so in a military way, while the Siamese were usually steadier and more persistent.

Hindu cultural traditions survived in both countries with equal vigor. Brahman priests were custodians of the ritual regalia at Court, and they supervised the ceremonies designed to sanctify newly accessioned rulers and to promote prosperity and order. Marriage ceremonies, where ritually observed, were also Hindu in character, since Buddhism negated such worldly attachments. The popular water festival, which was celebrated during the spring season, commemorated Indra's role as lord of the heavens, and the same Hindu influence was present in the ceremonial ritual plowing conducted by the Court. The white elephant veneration, which characterized the traditions of Mons, Burmans, Siamese, and Lao peoples, was of both Hindu and Buddhist origin. White elephants were considered omens of power and prosperity in Brahmanical lore, and were suggestive of Emergent Buddhas in light of the tradition that Gautama's progenitor had been such a creature. The systems of astrology and numerology practiced in Burma and Siam were also of Indian origin.

Commercial and economic factors contributed to important differences of outlook. The Burma of the Burmans was an inland kingdom, contemptuous of the value of foreign trade and harboring a traditional hostility toward the trading-minded Mon population of the delta regions. Economic isolation combined with distrust of outsiders generally contributed to the previously mentioned xenophobic aspects of the Burman point of view. The Siamese, by contrast, developed an active interest in overseas commerce, even though much of the trade of both Ayuthia and Bangkok was carried on by alien Chinese and the Dutch. Siamese forest products and rice, tin, and hides found ready markets in China and Japan. Most of the scores of Chinese-owned vessels operating out of Bangkok in the early nineteenth century were constructed of Siamese teak. The actual administration of the royal monopolies over coastal shipping and over particular commodities was usually sublet to Chinese bidders. Much the same was true with the collection of customs and taxes, and especially so under the Chakri dynasty after 1782.

Geographical location also contributed substantially to historical differences. British-Indian authorities who annexed Burma were not greatly interested in Siam either politically or commercially. Siam's general position on the eastern shores of the Indochina peninsula lay outside the security perimeter of India, as defined by the Calcutta authorities. Trade between Bangkok and the newly opened entrepôt of Singapore after 1820 ranked in volume second only to that of India itself, but virtually all of such Siamese trade was carried in Chinese-manned ships. The absence of British-Indian interference in Siamese affairs, including that of Bangkok's Malay sultanate vassals, was attributable in large measure to the overriding importance which Calcutta attached to the China trade. It was alleged, no doubt erroneously, that British interference with China's vassal Siam might disturb the lucrative trade with China. Unlike the isolationist rulers of interior Burma, Siam's government continued to be interested in commercial matters and free to conduct its foreign relations independently of the consent or the sufferance of the British-Indian authorities.

Early Rulers of the Chakri Dynasty

The first rulers of Siam's new Chakri dynasty, Rama I (to 1809) and Rama II (to 1821), followed an understandably cautious policy. They faced, down to 1802, the threat of major Burmese attacks, while the nuisance of Burmese-fomented subversion in Malaya continued as late as 1820. Rama I was able in 1795 to take advantage of the civil war in South Vietnam between the Tayson rebels and Prince Nguyen Anh to install as King of Cambodia a puppet Khmer prince named Anh Eng, who had previously been a refugee in Bangkok. Rama II, nevertheless, made no serious effort in 1812 to prevent the victorious Nguyen prince, now Emperor Gia Long, from establishing Vietnamese military ascendancy at Phnom Penh. Siam on this occasion was satisfied with compensatory gains at Cambodia's expense on the left bank of the Mekong River. Bangkok authorities were particularly wary in 1821 when John Crawfurd as head of a British diplomatic mission attempted in vain to obtain a treaty of commerce.

The accession of the strong-willed Prince Thap as Rama III in 1824 on the eve of the outbreak of the first Anglo-Burmese War afforded the Siamese government an opportunity to appraise anew the developing situation. The Siamese ruler was not unhappy to witness the development of the India-Burma conflict, for he expected to profit both in Tenasserim and in Malaya from the possible need by the British-Indian forces for Siamese aid. He wanted British authorities on Penang Island to surrender the defiant refugee Sultan of Kedah. He was also aware that the Tenasserim coast was not directly involved in the Anglo-Burman confrontation and might, therefore, constitute a bargaining issue. The wartime negotiations which Britain's Major Burney conducted at Bangkok were dragged out through 1825 and into 1826 awaiting military developments. When it became apparent in late 1825 that the British-Indian forces would need no assistance from Siam, Rama III rebuffed once more the British effort to conclude a comprehensive commercial treaty, demanding that British authorities not interfere with the dispatch by the Malay sultans of their customary vassalage missions to Bangkok and that the Sultan of Kedah be expelled from Penang. Siam advanced no claim to Tenasserim at the time for fear that such negotiations might involve making major concessions to Britain in Malaya. Except for the establishment of diplomatic relations and Siam's tacit recognition of the British lease of Penang from the Kedah Sultan, Major Burney's treaty of 1826 as a generally innocuous document.

The only treaty which Rama III took the initiative to conclude with any Western power during the course of his reign was with the American agent, Edmund Roberts, in 1833. It was virtually a carbon copy of the Burney treaty, but it did permit American commercial entry and the continued presence of the newly arrived American Protestant missionaries. Relations with the United States were apparently assumed by Rama III to be potentially advantageous because Americans had no colonial boundary claims to exploit and because they might become a source of firearms, as had been the case in previous American visits of 1818 and 1820. Few if any United States vessels touched at Siamese ports during the two succeeding decades.

Once the threat of future Burmese invasions was removed by the continuing British presence in Tenasserim, Rama III moved vigorously to consolidate Siam's control over border areas of Laos. He crushed a short-lived rebellion by Vientiane's Prince Anu in 1826-27 and proceeded to incorporate his domain into Siam proper. Rama III then extended effective suzerain control northward to Luang Prabang. He was eventually able in 1842, when Vietnam authorities were encountering trouble with the French navy, to cancel out the ascendancy which Gia Long had established at Phnom Penh in 1812. Bangkok's candidate, Ang Duong, was installed as Cambodia's King in 1842, and five years later Hué recognized his succession under the condition that Cambodia acknowledge the suzerainty of both neighbors. Rama III also reaffirmed Siam's nominal suzerainty over the Malay sultanates, and Penang did expel the Kedah Sultan, as promised in 1826. Thus in matters of governmental authority and border control, Siam was substantially stronger in 1850 than it had been in 1824.

Until the very end of Rama III's reign (1851), most of Bangkok's overseas trade continued to be carried by Chinese shippers, with Europeans having little share. In 1849, for example, several-score Chinese junks from Bangkok visited Singapore compared with only five British vessels calling at Bangkok. The royal coastal monopoly was strictly enforced around the Gulf of Siam and along the eastern shores of Malaya. The Siamese Court itself sent two heavily laden junks every year to Canton and a more pretentious semicommercial tributary mission to Peking every three years. Chinese merchants operating out of Bangkok enjoyed the best of both worlds in the China trade; they largely escaped the restrictive cohong system at Canton to which Europeans were subjected prior to the Opium War, and they also enjoyed greater privileges at Bangkok than were accorded Europeans. This was partly because Chinese agencies usually acted as Siam's tax farmers and customs collectors. Jealous Chinese merchants at Bangkok staged violent protests in 1837 and 1848 demanding the continuance of their privileged status. In 1850, Rama III flatly refused to liberalize Siam's traditional trading pattern as solicited by successive American and British missions. He saw no reason to do so, since the economy was prospering and a favorable trade balance was bringing silver into the country. The government's income in 1850 was approximately double what it had been at the time of Rama's accession in 1824.

By the end of the 1840s the Siamese king also began reacting negatively to the presence of Christian missionaries in his country, both French Catholic and Protestant American. Several Europeans were expelled, Siamese employees of missionaries were imprisoned, and a Protestant printing press was burned. The friction may have been aggravated by the too friendly relations, from the Court's point of view, between the foreigners and the Buddhist monk-scholar Prince Mongkut, whose claim to the throne had been passed over in 1824. The leader of the Catholic mission, Monsignor Pallegeoix, taught Mongkut Latin, and the American Reverend Jesse Caswell instructed him in English and in science. Caswell was permitted, in turn, to use monastery quarters in Bangkok for preaching and tract distribution. Mongkut was no monk in the traditional mold. He advocated Buddhist reforms in accordance with Mon and Sinhalese standards, developed an insatiable curiosity about Western science, and carried on a substantial correspondence with English-speaking friends. But the Court continued hostile to Westerners. Protests against Rama III's anti-foreign policies made by the American and British diplomatic missions which visited Bangkok in 1850 were completely ineffective, as were their efforts to establish consular relations and foreign residence and property rights.

Had Siam continued to pursue Rama III's policy of resisting European representations, the country would most probably have encountered in time the same irresistible military pressure which overtook its neighbors. Siam's nominal suzerain, China, had been forced by the treaty of Nanking to open its ports, to limit the scale of its customs duties, to accord extraterritoriality to foreign residents, and to admit the missionaries. In the light of the China precedent, neighboring minor states such as Siam could not expect to maintain for long their traditional royal trading monopolies and other restrictive regulations. It was under such threatening circumstances that the royal Senabodi Council of Siam selected in April 1851, as successor to the mortally ill Rama III, the reforming Prince-monk Mongkut, the student of Western science and the friend of scholarly foreigners.

Burma from Bagyidaw to Mindon

The standard of governing performance of Burma's kings since the first Anglo-Burmese War had gone from bad to worse. King Bagyidaw never recovered from the disgrace to himself and to his dynasty inflicted by defeat at the hands of British-Indian forces and the resulting punitive Yandabo treaty of 1826. His forces recovered control of Lower Burma from rebellious Mons and Karens, but he failed to achieve the expected return of Tenasserim Province in 1830 following his payment of the final installment of the war indemnity. Overwhelmed by melancholia and susceptible to periodic lapses from sanity, the King lost capacity to administer the government. Disorders engulfed the countryside. The contest for control between rival factions at Court was eventually resolved in 1838 by the accession of Prince Tharrawaddy, brother of the King, whose entourage included many bandit elements.

The early years of Tharrawaddy's short reign (1838-45) were occupied with the relocation of the capital from ill-omened Ava to nearby Amarapura and with the crushing of a Mon revolt. King Tharrawaddy flatly repudiated the Yandabo treaty and virtually forced the withdrawal of the British Resident from Mandalay by 1840. During this period of growing Burmese intransigence, the Siamese government communicated with British authorities in Tenasserim, offering military aid in the event that the British should be obliged to renew hostilities with Burma. From 1840 to 1842, it appeared that Burmese armies massed in Lower Burma might actually attack the British and the Siamese. This contingency was forestalled partly by Tharrawaddy's lapse into an insanity similar to the malady of Bagyidaw. Civil war eventually developed in 1844. This afforded opportunity for a palace coup engineered by Prince Pagan Min, who took over the kingdom from his father in the following year. Pagan proved to be avaricious of power, vengeful personally, and devoid of concern for good government. His five years of misrule came to an unlamented end in late 1852, during the course of the Second Anglo-Burman War.

The Anglo-Burmese war of 1852 developed from a minor incident involving British naval resentment over the levying by Rangoon authorities of a fine for alleged violation of port regulations. The initial British ultimatum was accepted by the unprepared Burmese government, but continued friction locally brought a second demand including a huge indemnity, which was completely unacceptable. When British occupation of key points in Lower Burma produced no conciliatory response, India's Governor-General Dalhousie proceeded to annex unilaterally all of the lower reaches of the Irrawaddy and Sittang valleys, a region possessing large agricultural and commercial potentials and also valuable teakwood forests. The forbidding prospect of a costly military campaign to force Amarapura's acquiescence in the British decision was obviated by the palace coup which brought to the throne Pagan's younger half-brother, Mindon Min, a long-time monk and a son of Tharrawaddy by an inferior queen. Backed by responsible elements of the Court, Mindon called off the Lower Burma war in favor of the pressing task of establishing order within his own domain. Burman resistance to British rule in Lower Burma degenerated into mere banditry after the withdrawal of Burmese officials and regular army contingents, although several years were required to bring disorders under control.

The handicaps which Mindon's Burma suffered as compared to Mongkut's Siam were formidable. They included a fragmented domain, a disorganized government, a discredited dynasty, a hard-pressed treasury, a disrupted economy, and serious limitations on Burma's freedom of diplomatic maneuver. Burma's only communications outlet lay through British-held territory, and British-Indian authorities discouraged direct contacts with London or with other foreign governments.

Personal Comparison of Mindon and Mongkut

King Mindon was generally recognized as a man of unquestioned integrity and sincerity. He was a remarkably even-tempered person, well intentioned, and incapable of trickery or deceit. His career prior to his accession to the throne was remarkable only in its demonstration of genuine religious commitment. His daily routine as King included prayer and scripture reading. He was reputedly interested also in the study of history, politics, geography, and philosophy, but his mind lacked the insatiable curiosity which characterized his Siamese counterpart. Mindon seems not to have developed any interest in the study of science as such and was not inclined to be critical of Buddhist religious standards of his time. One of his proudest accomplishments was his convening of the Fifth Great Buddhist Council and his inscription of the revised Tripitaka canon on the 729 marble slabs of Mindon's famous Kuthodaw monument at Mandalay. He did, however, initiate serious efforts to modernize his country and to reform his government. Although Mindon made no secret of his expectation that the British would eventually return Burma's captured provinces, whose loss he steadfastly refused to acknowledge by treaty, he nevertheless maintained friendly relations with successive British Commissioners of Lower Burma. He refused to take advantage of British embarrassments during the Crimean War, the Sepoy Rebellion, and the Second Anglo-Chinese War or to take sides in British involvements in Europe in the 1860s. It was Mindon's pattern which Premier Nu later attempted to emulate.

However much Mindon's authority was recognized by his revering people, his powers and his inclinations as King were narrowly circumscribed by traditional considerations as well as by immediate political factors. He had to contend with reactionary elements at the Court and also with quarreling relatives. Dissident leaders staged a dangerous palace coup in 1866, which resulted in the murder of the heir apparent and weakened the influence of the King by leaving in doubt the succession. Mindon was also destined to learn in time that continued good relations with British India were conditioned on the recognition of New Delhi's presumptive right to control Burma's foreign relations.

As previously indicated, Prince Mongkut was cast, by personality and training, in a less conventional mold than Mindon. His long term of twenty-seven years as a monk (1824-51) had been largely accidental. Although already married, he had entered the monastery at the age of twenty presumably for a limited period only. The sudden death of his father, Rama II, at this juncture and the selection by the Royal Council of his older and more experienced half-brother as the new King made inexpedient Mongkut's leaving of the monastery. Siam's monastic community at the time was at a low ebb in both discipline and morale, for it was recovering slowly from the demoralization experienced following the destruction of books and property in connection with burning of Ayuthia in 1767. Mongkut admired the superior discipline of an order of Mon monks, who had taken refuge in Siam from the wrath of the Burmese King. He wanted to eliminate adulterations which had crept into religious practices and to put a stop to the conducting of traditional rites mechanically and without proper understanding. His reform movement was intended, therefore, to revitalize the faith and to reject unauthentic tradition. He travelled widely through the Siamese countryside, visiting important shrines, including Ayuthia, and adopting from time to time the hermit's role of the forest dweller. Studying under leading Buddhist scholars, he mastered the Pali language and became by royal appointment head of the Board of Pali Examiners.

The influence of the Prince-monk was widely felt. He initiated the translation into Siamese of several-score ancient Pali manuscripts brought from Ceylon and also encouraged preaching in the Siamese language. With the aid of Western friends, he even undertook to study comparative religions. He recognized ethical similarities between Buddhism and Christianity but challenged as unscientific various aspects of Christian dogma and the miracle stories of the Bible. He was equally critical of Buddhist folklore which ran counter to reason. He nevertheless stopped short of creating a major schism.

Mongkut and Mindon as Rulers

Mindon and Mongkut differed somewhat in the depth of their reforming zeal, but even more in the atmosphere and circumstances at their respective courts which conditioned their efforts. Both rulers were perforce conservative and autocratic, taking full advantage of the aura of reverence attaching to their persons and to the traditional sanctions of divine kingship. Mongkut's coronation ceremonies in 1851, like those of his son and successor in 1868, included the ministrations of Brahmin experts in astrology and magic, the recitation of prayers to Śiva, the use of the sacred sword and white umbrella, and a lustral water bath. The rites concluded with the traditional circumambulation of the capital and preparations for the cremation of Rama III's remains. Mindon's coronation in 1853 followed precisely the same routine. But Mongkut was far more secure than Mindon in his actual authority, being able to enlist the services of able men, including princely brothers, in his governmental administration. Mongkut was also by nature more outspoken and self-reliant, and was freer to act and better informed about the outside world. The disorderly conditions which prevailed in Burma following Mindon's succession and again after a palace coup of 1866 were entirely absent in Siam. Mindon's financial problems were aggravated by his costly construction and embellishment of the new capital of Mandalay on an allegedly more prestigeful site, an action which was regarded as a political necessity, nevertheless.

The general atmosphere of the two Courts differed greatly with respect to their communication with outsiders, including Christian missionaries. Whereas Mindon could communicate only via an interpreter and by formal palace appointment, Mongkut conversed with Westerners frequently and informally. In order that his chief queens might share his facility in conversing with English-speaking visitors, the King enlisted the services of the wives of American missionaries over a three-year period as Court instructors in English. When Monsignor Pallegeoix returned to Europe on leave in 1852, he carried royal messages in Latin addressed to both Louis Napoleon and the Pope at Rome. Mongkut's vice-king and younger brother, Prince Chuda-muni, was even more competent in English than was the King, and he was also an avid devotee of applied science in such fields as navigation, telegraphy, iron casting, and steamboats. Chuda-muni named his eldest son Prince George Washington. No strong counter-influence existed at the Siamese Court capable of challenging the generally pro-Western inclinations of the King and his brother. Prince Chuda-muni died before Mongkut, paving the way for the succession of the latter's eldest son, Chulalongkorn, in 1868.

Reforming Efforts of the Two Rulers

If differences in timing and in the atmospheres of the two Courts are taken into account, the respective reforming accomplishments of the rulers were not greatly dissimilar. A number of Mongkut's initial innovations were symbolic rather than substantial, such as permitting subjects to approach him directly with petitions and foreigners at Court to stand upright in his presence. He also mitigated somewhat the status of debtor slaves, undertook to improve tax collections and the administration of justice, and encouraged the establishment of a Western-type school for sons of the nobility. But the essential charac-ter of Siam's government was little changed.

King Mindon meanwhile was unable to undertake reforming meas-ures until he cared for more urgent matters of state, such as restoring order, ending the British war, and relocating the capital. When he was finally able to move in 1858, he dispatched successive missions to Europe to bring back recommendations touching the solution of fundamental problems of government. In an effort to strengthen the central authority, both administratively and financially, Mindon undertook to eliminate feudal-type practices, such as the assignment of fief holdings to princes and high officials. In order to realize revenues sufficient to establish a system of regular salary compensa-tion for government officials, he imposed customs duties on trade with Lower Burma and a general household income tax based on a prosperity index regionally determined. The income tax proved diffi-cult to administer, because the officials could falsify the numbers of houses within their respective domains and customarily retained, without question, some 20 per cent of their collections. Tax revenues were never adequate to finance the salary program, so that abuses in the form of local exactions continued. Mindon later established ten new administrative posts charged with supervising the work of provincial governors and high-level judges.

Mindon's efforts extended also to the economic sphere. He introduced coined money in 1861, undertook to develop the mining of coal and iron, and even attempted to set up factories. His reform program received a major setback following the palace rebellion of 1866, previously mentioned. Traditionalists at Court thereafter were able to challenge the zeal of reforming elements and to take advantage of the weakened position of the King himself. Part of Mindon's financial difficulties were attributable to the large sums spent in connection with the convening of the Fifth Great Buddhist Council and the building of Mandalay. Expensive pagodas were constructed in the vicinity of Mandalay Hill, and Mindon contributed a new bejewelled *hti*, or pinnacle umbrella, to the tip of Rangoon's Shwe Dagon spire. After relations with British India worsened in 1872, the reforming party at the Court was thrown clearly on the defensive.

King Mongkut's contemporaneous widely heralded use of foreign experts in support of governmental reform reflected quite as much concern for diplomatic considerations as for reform *per se*. Mongkut was always careful, for example, to assign certain important responsibilities to British advisers. In addition to the tutors for the palace princes, these posts included the harbormaster, commander of the special police force recruited in Singapore, and financial adviser. Frenchmen served as Siam's legal advisers; Danes as bandmasters and drillmasters of the armed forces. An American usually headed the customs service, and another presided over King's College, which was established for the sons of the nobility. Engineers were drawn from a variety of European countries, including Prussia, in order to construct roads, bridges, canals, and telegraph lines, to establish a mint, and to prepare a dictionary. Resident Chinese maintained their traditional control over tax collection agencies and over royal monopolies covering the sale of opium and spirits.

The actual accomplishments of the foreign experts brought in by King Mongkut were substantially less than has sometimes been assumed. Bangkok itself acquired new facilities, but the Western innovations extended little beyond the confines of the capital. Rural Siam continued much as before. External trade increased in volume, but only in accordance with the upward trend already operative before the foreign experts arrived on the scene. The absence of substantial economic development within Siam has been attributed to insufficient state revenues. Under treaties concluded after 1855, tax assessments on foreign-owned properties were nominal. Foreign observers at the time appreciated Mongkut's interest in Western ways and his capacity for independence of thought, but they also deprecated his greed for power and his irritability and petulance, which were increasingly in evidence near the end of his reign. His unchallenged authority was frequently despotic and occasionally capricious. His reforming efforts were usually described as superficial, good only as far as they went.

King Mindon's corresponding efforts to obtain the services of foreign advisers, although belatedly undertaken and largely unsuccessful, were nevertheless persistent. His first attempt to strengthen his dispirited army was entrusted to a former officer of the British Indian forces. It ran aground on the impossibility of procuring the needed arms from British sources. Mindon made, in 1854, an abortive effort to establish diplomatic relations with the United States by sending with a returning missionary a letter to President Pierce requesting the establishment of treaty relations. The gesture was acknowledged, but Washington understandably at the time was not interested. Some success was achieved from 1855 to 1859 in the enlistment of French advisers for Burma as a result of an exchange of missions. A number of skilled French artisans and engineers passed through Rangoon in 1859 en route to Mandalay, bringing with them a river steamer designed for Burmese use on the Irrawaddy. British authorities at the time expressed concern that the objective of the French mission was mainly to encourage Mandalay to resist British demands. This early French involvement faded quickly when Louis Napoleon's interest was diverted to Italy and later to Mexico. When Burmese efforts to obtain French and Italian advisers were revived in the 1870s, British authorities at Rangoon regarded the proposal as a semblance of treason. By that time, Burma was becoming involved in a contest between European rivals for commercial access to western China.

Efforts to Establish Diplomatic Relations

The most striking differences between the performances of Kings Mongkut and Mindon were related to their success in establishing diplomatic relations. Mongkut was willing and able to act independently. Being aware of the growing importance of British influence in Eastern Asia, as demonstrated in the China war and in nearby Burma, he recognized that an accommodation would have to be made. Even so, the initiative came from Sir John Bowring, the British Governor of Hongkong and diplomatic plenipotentiary for Eastern Asia, who wrote to Mongkut from Singapore in 1854 while returning from leave in England. Mongkut invited Bowring to come to Bangkok to negotiate as representative of the British Crown, suggesting that both

American and French representatives might wish to accompany him. In the famous Bowring Treaty of 1855, fashioned free from coercive threats, Bangkok undertook to meet the essential demands of the West. These included extraterritorial rights, free access to Siamese ports, property rights under limited tax liability, freedom of interior travel, and nominal customs duties. Contemporaneous French negotiations conducted by Consul Montigny of Shanghai involved a gratuitous attempt to communicate with Cambodia, Siam's vassal, but this attempt was effectively sabotaged by Bangkok. Nevertheless, a treaty pattern acceptable to the West was established, and during the ensuing decade similar agreements were negotiated with five other Western states. Siam's independent status was thus widely acknowledged even though accomplished at considerable cost.

The kingdom of Burma sustained serious handicaps in its comparable efforts to gain similar recognition. Its outside relations were compromised from the very outset of Mindon's reign by the unilateral British annexation of Burma's lower Irrawaddy and Sittang valley outlets. British-Indian authorities tended, tacitly from the outset but overtly after 1867, to treat Burma as a minor Indian principality whose outside contacts could properly be supervised or inhibited. Even so, for the better part of two decades, friction was minimal. Mindon established relations of mutual respect during the first decade of his reign with such scholarly British Commissioners as Henry Yule and Arthur Phayre. The British Residency at Mandalay was reestablished in 1862. Some difference developed over Mindon's assessment of customs levies on trade with British Lower Burma, but the tax was explained as being intended for revenue purposes only and not for the curtailment of commercial relations. The Burma government purchased from the British several river steamboats designed to facilitate trade. In the treaty of 1867, King Mindon accorded full extraterritoriality to British residents in the kingdom of Burma plus free use of the Irrawaddy River throughout its navigable length up to Bhamo near the China border. Mindon demonstrated as much interest in the opening of the China trade as did the Rangoon merchants. He cooperated in the successful penetration of the rebel Panthay (Muslim) territory in Yunnan by the British Resident at Mandalay, Colonel Sladen, in 1868, and accorded the same generous support to the ill-fated Margary-Browne expedition into Yunnan in 1874-75. Such cooperation profited Burma very little in the end.

Divergencies with British Burma developed from political and commercial considerations outside Mandalay's control. During the disturbing episode of the palace coup of 1866 and the disorders which followed, several of the rebel princes took refuge in British Burma and later in India. British opposition to Burma's independence hardened perceptively in 1867-68 in the atmosphere of increasing imperialist rivalry with France which followed the Lagrée-Garnier exploration of the Mekong valley sponsored by French naval authorities at Saigon. British political and commercial spokesmen in Rangoon became convinced of the necessity of establishing direct contact with China via Upper Burma unless they were prepared to concede eventual French dominance over Yunnan's supposedly valuable trade. Distrust of French intentions eventually included those of the Burmese government as well. Of historical significance is the fact that Siam was not involved in this particular aspect of European rivalry because the favored route of access to Yunnan from the east was not via the nonnavigable Mekong River but up the Red River valley of Tongking.

The efforts of the Burmese government to escape from the tightening embrace of British-Indian commercial and diplomatic control during the final years of King Mindon were ineffectual. A high-ranking Burmese diplomatic mission which was sent to Europe in 1872 managed to negotiate two innocuous commercial treaties with France and with newly unified Italy, but the delegation was systematically boycotted by the British Foreign Office. The distinguished Burman leader of the mission brought back an ambitiously conceived plan for constitutional and administrative reform, along with proposals to send Burmese youth abroad to study, but opportunity was never afforded him to implement such ideas. Negotiations with France were renewed when a Paris emissary visited Mandalay in 1873 to exchange ratification of the commercial treaty. Secret Burmese proposals were then advanced to obtain the services of French officers to train the Burma army and to extend French good offices in the event of a third-power dispute involving Mandalay, but formal agreement was not forthcoming. With France distraught politically and still subjected at the time to the occupation of Prussian troops, the government of the anti-imperialist Premier de Broglie had neither the freedom nor the inclination to grant assistance to Burma. Rumors were nevertheless circulated at Rangoon at the time picturing Italian and French agents about to take over Mandalay, while in fact the discouraging atmosphere within the city was aggravated by the failing health of the monarch, uncertainties of succession, and the growing assertiveness of the traditionalist anti-reforming elements at Court.

In 1874, British-Indian authorities precipitated a break in diplomatic communications with King Mindon by refusing any longer to abide by established rules of Court etiquette calling for the removal of shoes by those entering the royal audience chamber. British commercial pressure to obtain at Burma's expense unimpeded access to Chinese Yunnan in competition with French efforts via Tongking mounted steadily. Time thus ran out on Mindon's persistent efforts to initiate reforms and to avoid, short of surrendering Burma's sovereign independence, giving offense to British-Indian authorities.

Successor Rulers in Burma and Siam

Following Mindon's death in September 1878, the struggle between progressive and reactionary elements of the Burmese Court was violently joined. Reforming elements undertook to revamp the administrative and fiscal structure along European cabinet lines, but the new youthful King Thibaw fell under the control of the opposing palace clique. A gruesome blood bath ensued, involving the death of several-score royal relatives and affording plausible grounds for British intervention. The immediate Burma crisis of 1878-79 passed because the British were involved at the time in Balkan affairs, in Afghanistan, and in South Africa. Thus the kingdom of Burma survived for another seven years, but only on sufferance. Its final absorption into British India in 1885 came after the French had actually occupied Tongking and were extending their interests into Laos. The immediate occasion for the British takeover was the levying of an exorbitant Burmese fine on a British firm accused of extracting timber illegally from across the Burma border. The fine was apparently occasion rather than cause.

Thus did Burma and Siam under Kings Mindon and Mongkut come historically to a parting of the ways. The former experienced as a part of India the full impact of the stridently modernizing but disruptive effects of colonial rule, while Siam managed to preserve essential aspects of its cultural vitality and political sovereignty. The principal reasons for the divergence are to be found elsewhere than in the personalities and reforming efforts of the two monarchs. Mindon's efforts at reform were frustrated in part by domestic political complications and in part by the lack of British cooperation with his endeavors. Such cooperation was denied despite his granting of free commercial access and extraterritorial privileges fully comparable to those accorded by Mongkut's treaties of 1855-56. Crucially important was the circumstance that Burma's territory lay adjacent to British India, within the perimeter of India's security concern, and athwart the only feasible route of access commercially from the Bay of Bengal to western China. Mongkut's son and successor, King

Chulalongkorn, although in many respects a more enlightened ruler than his father, proved quite ineffective in blocking later French imperialist designs in the Mekong valley region, except as he was able to balance off French designs against the economic stake which Britain had developed after 1855 in Siam proper. No comparable counterweight was available to Burma in resisting absorption by British India.

SIX

The Impact of Colonial Rule

Down to 1825, none of the four Buddhist nations of Southeast Asia was greatly affected by the presence of European commercial and naval influence in the region. Burma was the first to feel the impact, in peripheral areas at the outset, but eventually in the totality of its territory and social context. The process ended with its becoming an integral part of the Indian Empire. The timely diplomatic concessions made by King Mongkut, already described, moderated disturbing aspects of Western influence as far as Thailand was concerned. Cambodia fell under French protection in the early 1860s and Laos in the 1890s, both actions being taken as projections by French colonial authorities of their inherited suzerain status previously enjoyed by Vietnam. The results of the colonial impact were highly varied both in degree and in kind, creating differences which carried over into the postwar independence period of the 1940s and 1950s.

The British Role to 1870

The British occupation of the lower Burma Tenasserim coast from Moulmein to Tavoy in 1825 contributed at the outset distinct advantages to the local population. The Tenasserim corridor between Burma and Siam had been used innumerable times by contending armies, both Burmese and Siamese, to the great distress of the resident Mon and Karen peoples. British occupation meant the end of military intrusions and arbitrary extortions and the establishment of general security for lives and property. During the initial decade of the occupation, British authorities worked out an adaptation of customary law, utilized indigenous leadership, and made salaried administrative agents out of the headmen. Slavery was abolished in line with the Act of the London Parliament of 1833. Coined money was introduced, and trade was greatly expanded. Difficulties developed in the collection of per capita tax assessments and in the exaction of forced labor for the building of unwanted roads. The resulting practice of importing convict labor from India contributed to disorder during the early thirties.

The increasing Indianization of governmental administration in Tenasserim began in 1835 in respose to the unofficial demand for the establishment of formal court procedures, operating under Indian law and utilizing professional legal counsel. The new system destroyed the customary basis of land usage and served to undermine family and village cohesion and social vitality within the area. Disorders led to abuses of administrative authority by British Company officials. When an overscrupulous Commissioner attempted in 1846 to curb the irregular activities of British timber merchants, his dismissal was promptly obtained. The economic results of British control were, nevertheless, clearly positive. From 1835 to 1852, the population of Tenasserim multiplied two and one-half times.

The impact of British control in the Arakan district of Burma differed substantially from that in Tenasserim. Arakan lay adjacent to coastal Bengal, and it had been a part of the Burma kingdom only since 1784. The easy introduction of cheap Bengali labor, along with Indian capital and orderly British rule, made possible a rapid increase in rice production and export. An American visitor to the port city of Akyab in 1834 reported that Hindustani was the *lingua franca*. Indigenous protests against the process of Indianization were completely ineffectual.

The arbitrary reduction of the status of the traditional Arakanese headmen to the role of salaried clerks or mere tax collectors stirred an abortive rebellion in 1836. The vastly improved economic situation operated in time to quiet unrest, and Arakan began to attract emigrant cultivators from independent Burma. Rice acreage under cultivation multiplied nearly five times during the period from 1826 to 1852. By 1836, the treasury of the East India Company was profiting in Arakan to the extent of some 600,000 rupees annually, while the identity of the traditional kingdom, for better or for worse, was being obliterated.

British annexation in 1852 of the lower reaches of the Irrawaddy and Sittang valleys of Burma proper, filling in the coastal gap between Arakan and Tenasserim provinces, posed a somewhat different administrative problem. The inability of the Burmese forces to stem the well-executed British-Indian invasion led to the palace coup which replaced King Pagan with King Mindon, as was discussed in Chapter Five. Virtually all high Burmese officials, both civilian and military, retired northward to the remnant of independent Burma when the war came to an end, leaving a vacuum of indigenous leadership in Lower Burma. Resistance raised by retainers of the Burman *myothugyi* headmen who remained behind modulated from rebellion to mere banditry with the passage of time. Political disaffection persisted to 1857, and widespread lawlessness continued in Lower Burma until 1870.

The traditional structure and sanctions of governmental authority, both central and local, disintegrated during the period of disorder. The emerging alien policing and court system was popularly unintelligible, while customary restraints on conduct, including religious sanctions, lost their potency. Efforts were made with limited success to use cooperative individuals of influence as township officials for tax collections and the trial of petty criminal cases. Village police officers (*gaungs*), charged with enforcing British-Indian law, lost entirely their traditional *rapport* with the people. Bad manners displaced traditional respect for elders, as many of the youth became arrogant and bullying, especially in the newer communities which grew up in localities adjacent to areas of expanding rice cultivation.

The new colonial administrative system had its positive and integrative aspects as well. The three parts of British Burma were amalgamated in 1862 into the equivalent of a Commissioner's province of India, although for some 35 years thereafter it lacked legislative autonomy. Systematic land surveys provided, after 1877, a dependable and relatively equitable basis for land tax assessments. Responsible British Deputy Commissioners drawn from the India civil service were placed in charge of the administrative districts where they exercised plenary executive and administrative authority. The combined effects of orderly administration and economic incentives accomplished, even before the opening of the Suez Canal in 1869, a substantial improvement in Lower Burma's prosperity. Trade and population within the region doubled between 1853 and 1865, while rice acreage under cultivation tripled by 1872. Increasing rice surpluses found a ready market in India. Steam navigation dominated the Irrawaddy traffic; railway lines were built northward to Prome on the Irrawaddy and to Toungoo on the Sittang River. The expanding industry of teakwood extraction was placed under strict governmental supervision. All of this was preliminary to the real economic boom which followed in the 1870s as a result of the opening of the Suez Canal.

Along the rapidly expanding agricultural frontier of Lower Burma's Irrawaddy delta and the Sittang valley, the abandonment of the traditional principle of the extended-family ownership of land in favor of individual ownership had disturbing social consequences. Tax receipts for the payment of the nominal initial assessments on newly developed land were recognized after 1876 as presumptive evidence of ownership. Such receipts became, therefore, acceptable as collateral for mortgage loans which were subject to foreclosure in case of payment default. This procedure—novel for Burma— played into the hands of the usurer, often Chinese or Indian, and led in time to widespread land alienation and to an enormous volume of court litigation connected with the transfer of land titles. Money borrowed at high cost was often spent for uneconomic ends. The alien legal system which British-Indian courts applied became mainly an instrument of profit for lawyers and moneylenders.

The Burmese pioneers who engaged in the process of agricultural development, an increasing number of them migrants from Upper Burma, lacked social stability as a result of their being constantly on the move. The conduct of such persons was frequently not amenable to local community control or to the traditional ethical sanctions based on religious considerations. The characteristic poverty of the borrowing cultivator was aggravated in Lower Burma by the suspension of traditional sumptuary laws regulating proprieties of dress, housing, and the accouterments accorded to recognized social status. Crime suppression became increasingly ineffective because the evidence obtainable in court was usually fallacious and perjury indictments were difficult to prove.

The one factor more than any other which held society together in the face of growing individualism was continuing popular adherence to the Buddhist religion. Reverence for the yellow-robed monk, the sacredness of pagoda premises, the persistence of the traditionalist amalgam of Buddhist worship and spirit propitiation remained stubbornly impervious to alien cultural influences. Continued adherence to Buddhist tradition became progressively the essential surviving characteristic of Burman national identity. This was true in spite of the widening of sect differences within Lower Burma, where an authoritative referee no longer existed to resolve religious disputes. Efforts of the government to modernize the monastic schools by introducing new curricula and by improving instruction accomplished very little. That fraction of the Burman urban elite who were educated in the new lay government schools were usually drawn into government and into the legal profession. They, thus, became somewhat Western-oriented, but seldom in a thoroughgoing way.

This exaggerated emphasis on Buddhist sentiment as the essential factor in national cohesion raised grave problems in time. The very potency of such Buddhist adherence, combined with an increasing lack of discipline within monastic ranks, produced monk-led violence after 1886. It led eventually to the rise in power of the sinister and politically demogogic *pongyi*, who became increasingly influential in the 1920s. This group tended to cast aside traditional Buddhist rules forbidding concern with mundane affairs and undertook actively to foment rebellion along partisan religious lines. Monastic politicians were destined later to revive their disruptive role within the Union of Burma during the 1950s by challenging the idea of a secular state and other modernizing trends. Burma's postwar efforts to adjust to the outside world were thus gravely handicapped by the association of national identity with the persistence of religious tradition, even though the latter had provided an effective integrative cultural factor during the course of the colonial period.

British Rule from 1870 to 1889

As previously suggested, the period of the 1870s which followed the opening of the Suez Canal witnessed a rapid acceleration of Burma's economic development. Easier access to European markets for bulky commodities, such as rice and timber, also stimulated intra-regional trade as well. British employer groups, both government and private, annually brought over to Burma increasing numbers of Indian coolie laborers, who built the docks, the railroads, and the roads and manned the processing facilities. Coolie laborers also helped in the seasonal planting and harvesting of the paddy crop. The money needed for such economic growth was provided and distributed by the Chettyar moneylender caste of Madras, who maintained a close working connection with Calcutta banks.

The accelerated pace of economic growth owed much to the increasingly aggressive mood of the British business community at Rangoon. This mood expressed itself in the growing impatience with the continued existence of the interior Burmese state, which appeared to constitute a barrier to future British access to the trade of western China, trade which was in competition with the French from Tongking. The consequent British opposition to King Mindon's efforts to extend Burma's diplomatic relations was described in Chapter Five. Another effect of the accelerated economic tempo and the presence of alien Indian laborers in considerable numbers was the increased incidence of lawlessness and the general social disintegration which was prevalent throughout Lower Burma.

For various reasons, the British authorities at Rangoon failed to exploit the opportunity, which was afforded them by the excesses of the Mandalay Court during the early years of King Thibaw's rule, to liquidate the Kingdom of Burma. The stage for intervention was originally set during the summer of 1879. A major deterrent factor was the outbreak in early autumn of a British war in Afghanistan on the opposite western borders of India. This incident was followed by the development of strife with the Boers in South Africa and by the accession in 1880 of the anti-imperialist Gladstone as Prime Minister at London. Gladstone remained in power until June 1885. Unfortunately for King Thibaw, the reform faction at his Court was unable to take advantage of the five-year leeway thus granted them to improve the character of their government. Instead, corruption became increasingly rampant, lawless bands began roaming the countryside, and formidable rebellions developed in the Shan states and the Kachin country.

During the course of this five-year interim, official French interest in Buddhist Southeast Asia increased. The province of Tongking was annexed by France following a brief war with China, and the French admirals who were directing Indochina policy laid claim to whatever suzerain rights the Vietnamese had previously exercised in the Laos country. One consequence of revived French interest was its development of diplomatic relations with Mandalay, to the exaggerated alarm of British commercial interests at Rangoon. The matter came to a head in 1885 when, following the negotiations at Paris of a Burma-French commercial treaty, a French representative journeyed to Mandalay to exchange ratifications. On his own initiative, he proceeded to initial a new capital-aid agreement which was potentially political in character. Although this unauthorized French *rapprochement* was repudiated by Paris following protest from London, the situation provided a suitable context for increasing British alarm over the presumed abuse of Burma's diplomatic freedom to negotiate outside the scope of British-Indian suzerainty.

The occasion for the destruction of the Kingdom of Burma came in late 1885, in connection with the levying of an exorbitant fine by the Burma government on a British timber firm whose operations extended across the boundary above Toungoo. The alleged offense of the firm was violation of Burmese regulations covering logging-extraction operations. The timber-firm crisis developed during a brief six-months interim when Gladstone was out of power, from June 1885, to January 1886. An ultimatum was issued in late October calling, among other things, for Mandalay's assignment to British-

Indian authorities of control over Burma's foreign relations. Burma's feeble and unprepared forces proved entirely unable to resist the ensuing invasion. The capital of Mandalay was occupied, and the captured King Thibaw was transported to Madras.

Both the initiative to invade Burma and the decision concerning its disposition were primarily the concern of the British-Indian authorities. The question of whether to install a puppet prince or to annex the kingdom outright was decided in part by the absence of any really acceptable royal candidate. The alternative of annexation was also supported by Calcutta's mistaken idea that, in view of the ease of the conquest, the incorporation of Upper Burma would not entail any great difficulty. As anticipated by Britain's Commissioner Charles Bernard and other officials acquainted with Burma, a prolonged period of rebellion ensued. It started as mere banditry and anarchy, often pitting village against village. But following the public announcement, made in late February 1886, that the monarchy would not be revived and that all of Burma would become a part of British India, guerrilla operations developed formidable political overtones. The elimination of the royal Court meant for most Burmans the sacrifice of their identity as a people and the elimination of any governmental support of customary law and the Buddhist faith. British-Indian pacification operations continued for almost five years and involved the use of some 32,000 Indian troops and the support of a larger number of Burman police. The total cost, borne by India, was more than ten times the original estimates. British use of irregular Karen police, Christian-led, in opposition to pongyi-led Burman rebels stimulated Karen national consciousness and sowed the seeds of later strife. The provision of employment for restive Burmans in the construction of the Toungoo branch of the railway northward to Mandalay, however, helped finally to divert attention from political grievances.

The pacification of peripheral areas of Burma was accomplished with relative ease. Inter-state strife between the Shan State princedoms was brought to an end by 1888 through negotiations with the leading Sawbwa princes, whose traditional authority was fully confirmed. The Kachin tribesmen of northern Burma also agreed, in 1892, to submit their internal disputes to British adjudication. A similar agreement with the Chin tribesmen of the Manipur border area was concluded in 1895. The boundary with Siam was drawn in 1892, and four years later the upper Mekong River was accepted as the border between French Laos (above Siam) and the easternmost Shan states. The French also agreed in 1896 to refrain from extending their colonial influence into the central Menan valley area of Siam.

The Revised Pattern of British Administration

The principal change introduced in the British administration of Burma by Commissioner Charles Crosthwaite, who took over in 1889, related to the elevation of the village headman to semiofficial status and to the assignment to him of onerous responsibilities. The headman served as the local police officer, as petty magistrate, as enforcer of health regulations, and as tax collector, for which duties he was compensated by the retention of ten per cent of his cash collections. He was also empowered to exact *corvée* labor from male villagers for the maintenance of wells, roads, and the night watch. Although generally responsible to the District Deputy Commissioner and his township assistants, the headman after the turn of the century was also obliged to maintain contact with specialized governmental agencies such as the judiciary and public works, health, and police officials. Execution of such a variety of duties proved to be beyond the competence and acknowledged authority of most headmen, and performance was consequently minimal. In order to provide more adequate compensation for such work, the village units were later broadened, so that the total number of village units was reduced by approximately one-third.

The new system worked fairly well for several decades in Upper Burma, where village communities were fairly stable and most of the land was still owned by large family groups. Once the rebellion in this region subsided, traditional mores regained vitality, and order was restored. In Lower Burma, by contrast, the system usually failed to maintain order, especially in the newer communities. Local youth tended to disregard the authority of the headman, and family solidarity was not effective as an element of control. Expansion of rice acreage at an average of more than 100,000 acres per year was accomplished for the most part by cultivator tenants who were up to their ears in debt to moneylenders and who shifted endlessly from one bankrupt holding to another. Forced to compete in agricultural off-seasons with coolie laborers from India, many Burmans preferred to spend part of the year as participants in lawless gangs. Prior to this time, such lawless epidemics had occurred only during periods of enfeebled royal control. Policing efforts to curb criminal activity were generally ineffective, partly because the basic causes of social disintegration lay beyond the control of the police and partly because accurate court testimony was difficult to obtain; bribery of both police and lower court officials became epidemic. A perceptive British Settlement Department officer aptly characterized the resulting situation as "anarchy boxed in."

In time a semi-Westernized Burmese elite developed and filled the class level between the village headman and the upper strata of British officials. This indigenous elite managed to qualify for Class II civil service, for the legal profession, or for positions as teachers in the Anglo-vernacular schools, both missionary and government-sponsored. As a class, the English-trained group shared little in common with the untutored villager, apart from their continuing attachment to Buddhist practices and affiliations. The elite was, for the most part, a self-seeking rather than self-sacrificing group, very much as the traditional Court clientèle had been. Associated with them were several Burmese landowners and rice mill operators. A middle-class business stratum failed to emerge mainly because the tradition was lacking and the Burmese faced strenuous economic competition from alien Chinese and Indian business elements of the population. The population as a whole shared sparingly in the profits of expanding production. The ablest member of the Burman elite attained the rank of Deputy Commissioner by 1908, and another was accorded a position as judge of the High Court by 1917. The first appointed Legislative Council of 1897, advisory in character, contained one Burman and one Shan. When the Council was expanded in 1909, thirteen non-British representatives were included in the total of thirty members.

The social and cultural consequences of British elimination of the traditional Burman elite, from the King down to the *myothugyi*, and the substitution of a quasi-Anglicized upper crust were serious and cumulative. The change deprived the society as a whole of leaders possessing the traditional symbols of authority, of those capable of determining taste in manners and fashions, and of patrons of literature, art, and religion. Expert craftsmanship died. So did the high level of competence in the Burmese language. The children of socially aspirant families attended Anglo-vernacular schools (often missionary), while Hindustani became the *lingua franca* of the urban marketplace. The erosion of monastic discipline, especially following the government's failure to replace the last presiding bishop (*thathanabaing*) in 1895, was aggravated by the widening cultural barriers and a resurgence of primitive magic and spirit cults. The traditional conservatism of Buddhism prevented its leadership from contributing anything to the needed adjustment to Westernizing influences. As in the case of social disintegration, evidence of cultural decline was less apparent in Upper Burma, and for the same reason that disruptive influences there were less potent. Another unfortunate aspect of cultural transition was the frustration experienced by many students. They were obliged to study in a strange language, which caused them to suffer a high proportion of failures in their exams, and to compete in the end for a limited number of civil service posts. Many of them, meanwhile, became contemptuous of the older Buddhist-centered disciplines and were no longer amenable to parental control.

If British Burma suffered losses in terms of social disintegration and cultural decline as compared with its Buddhist neighbors, it gained very substantially in economic development. The average annual increment in rice cultivation during the fifteen years prior to 1870 had been an impressive 50,000 acres; the rate more than doubled during the two succeeding decades. The impetus came from the expanded market of the triangular trade pattern between Burma, India, and Europe, a market in which British and Indian merchants took the lead. Experienced cultivators from Upper Burma, along with Indian labor and Chettyar capital, cooperated in British Burma to promote rice production. The Burma government provided internal transportation and docking facilities, and also constructed bunds needed for water control throughout the delta area. The annual delta monsoon rainfall of around 110 inches from June through September was normally sufficient to provide adequate water for wet-rice cultivation, although destructive floods and occasional droughts at the end of the growing season could cause heavy crop damage. The government also provided a legal framework for handling the tide of litigation relating to the transfer of land titles and kept a careful record of landholdings through the Settlement Department. At the same time, substantial increases in cotton and oil seed production occurred in Upper Burma, and sugar cane growing was expanded in the middle Sittang valley. Commercial agriculture emerged quickly to dominate Burma's economy.

Few of the Burmese pioneers who cleared Lower Burma's virgin lands with the aid of borrowed funds were able to occupy their holdings for the twelve years necessary for the acquiring of full title. Crop failure, improvident spending, high interest rates, and vagaries of the market contributed to the land alienation problem. Occasional trade recessions (as in 1894 and 1907-8) aggravated agricultural distress even in Upper Burma. From the 1880s on, both the Chettyars and the cultivators suffered from collusive buying practices on the part of the British milling firms. Except for oil and timber extraction, few Burmans benefited from the nonagricultural growth of the economy, which expanded to include, in time, mining in the northern Shan States (lead, zinc, silver), wolfram extraction to the east of Toungoo, river and railway transportation, cement plants, and some rubber plantations. The Burman cultivator usually did not go hungry, but he profited little from his endeavors. Competition with Chinese innkeepers, traders, and artisans, and with Indian coolies, moneylenders, merchants, and professional men was difficult for Burmese peoples to match. The British business community, which alone was adequately represented in the advisory legislative Council, was not inclined to tackle the difficult task of halting land alienation. The British found it easier to espouse the laissez faire assumption that the advantages of increased productivity would automatically over the long-run benefit the population generally. Apart from the starting of several hundred Cooperative Credit Societies after 1910, no real efforts were made to cope with this problem. The British authorities, backed by the enormous financial and military resources of the Indian Empire, did not admit the need for any substantial reforms in the years prior to World War I.

French Rule in the Lower Mekong Valley

As previously suggested, French rule over Laos and Cambodia developed legally as a projection of inherited suzerain authority which had previously been exercised by the Vietnamese kingdom of Annam. The French takeover, which was accomplished during the twenty-five years after the first tenuous French foothold was acquired at Saigon in 1859, had considerable historical weight behind it. French missionary interest in the region dated from the time of Louis XIV, but more tangible political connections were established by the French vicar apostolic, Pigneau de Behaine, in the 1790s. By 1802, Pigneau and several of his fellow adventurers helped an exiled Nguyen prince to unify the country, and to assume his reign name as Emperor Gia Long. The French admiralty eventually developed an active interest in the Annamite coast during the reign of Gia Long's successor, King Minh Mang, in the 1830s, when periodic protests were registered against the persecution of Catholic missionaries by the increasingly suspicious Hué authorities. But Premier Guizot and King Louis Philippe were little interested. When Emperor Louis Napoleon ascended to power in France in 1851, missionary partisans gained a more sympathetic hearing in Paris than they had previously enjoyed.

Opportunity for vigorous action came in connection with French participation in the Anglo-Chinese War of 1858-60. In between the two phases of that war, while the Tientsin treaties were being returned to Europe for ratification, French naval forces, aided by a small Filipino contingent, landed at Tourane harbor (modern Da Nang) and made a futile attempt to force Hué to negotiate. Lacking the local Catholic cooperation promised by missionary sponsors and with serious illness developing among French forces, the Tourane effort ran entirely aground.

In a desperate effort to salvage something from the Tourane debacle, the commanding French admiral, Rigault de Genouilly, shifted his attack to the city of Saigon in the south. The citadel was captured in early 1859 and held precariously during the ensuing two years until the second phase of the China War was completed. Although Louis Napoleon by 1861 had lost interest in the discouraging Cochin-China adventure, the French admirals, whose reputations and honor were committed to achievement of victory, refused to abandon the enterprise. They first enlarged their holdings in the immediate vicinity of Saigon. In June 1862, they forced Hué authorities, who were distracted by the threat of a rebellion in Tongking on behalf of a rival dynastic contender, to acknowledge the loss of three Cochin-China provinces.

The next French advance was made in Cambodia. Under the convenient assumption of manifest destiny, French naval leaders, as presumed heirs of Vietnamese suzerainty, forced the feeble Cambodian ruler in 1863 to sign a secret treaty agreeing to surrender control of his country's foreign policy to France and to accept the presence of a French Resident at his capital at Phnon Penh. King Mongkut's protest from Bangkok was brushed aside when the treaty became public in 1864. Three years later Bangkok was persuaded to recognize Cambodia's vassalage to France in return for the compensatory concession that the border provinces of Siemreap (Angkor) and Battambang properly belonged to Siam. Later in 1867, the French admirals assumed control over the three remaining provinces of Cochin-China, ostensibly to forestall independent Vietnamese interference in the affairs of Cambodia. King Norodom was forced in 1884 to agree that a French administration paralleling his own should assume control. This in effect reduced the King to a mere symbol of nationhood and religion. Traditional social and political patterns were little disturbed. A brief protest rebellion followed. The two border provinces conceded to Siam in 1867 were later recovered for French Cambodia in 1907. French protection was accepted in

Phnom Penh as a substitute for the country's previous predicament of vassalage to both Hué and Bangkok.

Further extension of French interest in the Mekong valley came with the despatch of the famous Lagrée-Garnier exploring expedition in 1866-68. This expedition was a cooperative venture sponsored by the naval authorities at Saigon and by the Paris Geographical Society, whose president happened to be an ex-Minister of Marine. The principal objective of the endeavor was to determine whether the valley of the great river would provide a commercially feasible route to western China. In its initial stages of operation the party explored the ruins of ancient Angkor. They also discovered the turbulent, nonnavigable character of the river itself and the fact that the only really feasible trade route from Vietnam into Yunnan Province of China was via the Red River valley debouching at Hanoi in Tongking. Before the results of the expedition could be publicized by the surviving leader, Garnier, in his magnificent two-volume account, which was published in Paris by the Ministry of Marine in 1873, Louis Napoleon's regime had collapsed in the Franco-Prussian War. The feeble Third French Republic was occupied for four years by German troops. Paris peace negotiators were so uninterested in Indochina in 1871 that they suggested the possibility of giving Cochin-China to Germany as part of the indemnity. Bismark on the occasion declined the offer.

During the ensuing decade, the French naval commanders left in charge at Saigon could do little more than hold on grimly to their precarious position. An abortive intervention undertaken at Hanoi in 1873 involved the activities of a French merchant in the employ of the Chinese Governor of Yunnan and the daring seizure of the citadel by "mediating" French adventurers led by Garnier. The move had to be disavowed by Saigon on orders from Paris, but the episode did afford French authorities the opportunity to exact from the Annamite Court belated acknowledgment of French sovereignty over all of Cochin-China, plus the limited right of access to the Red River valley route for trading purposes. Garnier was killed during the escapade and became a martyr to the cause of French control over Tongking. During the decade of the 1870s, however, France was primarily occupied at home by the struggle between the partisans of monarchy and advocates of the republic.

In 1881 the French *mission civilisatrice* in Vietnam first became a serious concern at Paris. From 1881 to 1885 Minister Jules Ferry came to the aid of the navy at Saigon and attempted to popularize French expansion as a kind of patriotic duty. The apparent British intention to annex the Burma kingdom after 1879 stimulated French interest in Tongking, as part of the colonial rivalry to gain access to the presumed profitable trade with Yunnan.

The French forward move into Annam and Tongking began in 1881 on authorization from Jules Ferry. The city of Hanoi was occupied militarily in 1882 as were the coastal province of Nam Dinh and the neighboring coal fields of Hon-gay. The government at Hué was powerless to resist the assertion of French suzerainty, but trouble developed in 1883-84 between France and China. Vietnam had deliberately revived its traditional vassalage relationship to China in 1877. Chinese forces soon entered the upper portions of Tongking Province to challenge French control. The first round of negotiations at Tientsin, which was aimed at withdrawal of Chinese troops and Peking's acknowledgement of French suzerainty over Annam, was concluded in May 1884. But the negotiations were followed almost immediately by a revival of Chinese resistance locally. France was, therefore, committed to a brief but costly and highly unpopular war with China. The eventual conclusion of the supplementary treaty with China in March 1885, which conceded additional French commercial access to Yunnan up the Red River valley, did little to quiet the rising French criticism of Ferry and his aggressive policies. Ferry was accordingly forced out of office, and the French Chamber ratified the annexation of Tongking only by the narrowest of margins. Six months after Ferry fell from power, the British moved to take over Burma in pursuance of their own plans to obtain direct access to Yunnan.

As had been the case two decades earlier, the French naval officers left in control of the expanded Indochina possessions after 1885 were again accorded little backing from their home government. French political interest shifted back to Europe during the exciting period of the Boulanger crisis; imperialist interest tended to center in North Africa, and the distant and highly expensive Indochina venture came in for particularly vigorous criticism. Throughout the remainder of the 1880s and well into the following decade, Tongking continued in a state of chronic rebellion, while coastal Annam, although relatively quiescent, was decidedly uncooperative. The naval officers who continued to head the colonial government struggled in vain to set up an administration able to meet local needs and to supply the funds needed for both current expenses and economic improvements. A major step to correct the embarrassing situation was taken by Paris in 1887, when the previously combined Ministry of Marine and of Colonies was divided. Thereafter the Colonial au-

thorities were assigned responsibility for administering the four existing sections of French Indochina, Cochin-China, Cambodia, Annam,
and Tongking. The formal shift of control was accomplished in
1894, by a civilian Commissioner named J. P. de Lanessan who was
placed in charge of French Indochina in 1891.

At the time of his arrival, de Lanessan faced an almost desperate
situation of banditry and rebellion in the north, an uncoordinated
administrative structure for the area as a whole, and a woeful lack of
funds. His governmental reforms included the use of the traditional
Chinese mandarin system for Annam and Tongking under the direction of the Emperor at Hué and the improvement of the direct
French administration in Cochin-China. He almost doubled the
annual tax revenue receipts during his four-year term of office and
also raised substantial loans for improving docks and transport facilities. Little change or improvement was made in the Cambodian
protectorate, except in expanding transportation facilities and in
rebuilding the capital of Phnom Penh.

French Annexation of Laos, 1893 to 1907

As previously indicated, the Lao peoples occupying the Mekong
valley proper and its left-bank tributaries were associated historically
far more closely with the Siamese than with the Vietnamese living
beyond the mountains to the east. The Lao themselves were identical with the peoples of Chiengmai and Chiengrai inhabiting northwestern Siam, and were insulated from Vietnam by the interposition
of alien hill tribesmen of several varieties. As Theravada Buddhists,
the Lao used the Thai script and language, and cherished Indian
symbols of divine kingship, including the white umbrella and the
sacred white elephant. By contrast, the Chinese-type mandarin system of government and reverence for ancestral spirits and remains,
both prevalent in Annam, had little meaning to the Lao people.

After the withdrawal of the Burmese armies, in the 1580s, much
of the Lao country had been customarily vassal to Siam. One Hué-
supported prince was installed at Vientiane for a brief period after
1697, and again during the attacks on Ayuthia by Burma's Konbaung
dynasty in the 1760s. In 1778, Siam recovered a share in suzerainty
over Vientiane. In 1826, when the invading Vientiane prince was
defeated by Rama III, the former fled to Hué. Rama III proceeded
in 1836 to annex outright all Lao-inhabited areas on the left bank
of the Mekong adjacent to Vientiane and to strengthen the indirect
Siamese rule elsewhere in Laos. Thus when the newly arrived French
authorities in Annam and Tongking posed as the successor to Viet-

nam's suzerain rights in Laos, their historical and legal position was qualified at best. Siam's superior claim to Laos was, in fact, recognized implicitly in the French agreement made with Bangkok in 1885, when Siam consented to the establishment of a French vice-consulate at Luang Prabang.

The French acquisition of Laos was largely the work of the highly resourceful Consul, Auguste Pavie, who reached his post at Luang Prabang via Siam in May 1886. By siding with the Laotian King and — playing upon the local resentment of Siamese overlordship, Pavie solicited local acceptance of the alternative of French protection. Pavie was eventually transferred to Bangkok as French Minister in 1892, where he played a leading role in the French-provoked crisis of the following year. As a kind of last-effort expansionist move by the retiring naval authorities, a minor demand for reparations was authorized by Paris and magnified by Pavie and the fleet authorities into a French claim for a protectorate over the entire left bank of the Mekong River valley and for the removal of all defensive Siamese installations in the region. This sweeping demand was supported later by the unauthorized dispatch of French gunboats up the Menam River to Bangkok itself. When King Chulalongkorn learned that no direct assistance from Britain was available to counter French aggression, he had no alternative but to agree to the French demands regarding Laos. Britain's desire to safeguard Burma's claim to the easternmost Shan state of Kengtung bordering the upper Mekong River was reflected in a treaty with France negotiated in 1896. The treaty also exacted a French pledge not to interfere in the Menam valley of Siam proper, where British trade and investments were centered. Further surrenders of Siamese territorial claims to France in 1904 and 1907 included not only the provinces of Siem-reap and Battambang in Cambodia but also two smaller regions along the right bank of the Mekong above the great bend and westward to the watershed of the upper Menam. A final sacrifice of territory to colonial pressure came in 1909, when Siam's tenuous suzerain claims to four northern Malay sultanates were surrendered in return for a substantial British railway loan.

The general acceptance by the Laotian peoples of French colonial control can be explained primarily by the fact that this control entailed a minimum of interference with traditional customs or political institutions. The prerogatives of the King at Luang Prabang were fully honored by the French. Preference was also given to the princely elite groups in the selection of officials in the three other politically defunct states of Champassak, Vientiane, and Xieng

Khoung. External interference by Siam and Vietnam was cancelled, and internal tribal tensions were balanced off. Three isolated Montagnard rebellions were put down between 1901 and 1921. Vientiane, the administrative capital, was under the rule of a French *Resident Superieur,* who exercised direct control in areas outside Luang Prabang proper, but according to traditional patterns of authority. The French administration encountered strenuous objections, however, from the Lao when Vietnamese were brought in as subordinate officials and when annexation of parts of Laos to Tongking was proposed. Abolition of slavery also aroused a rebellion on the part of slave-trading Kha tribesmen in southern Laos. French officials continued to supervise financial affairs and to maintain essential health services, but in policing and court matters they made full use of the traditional authority of the native chiefs. The French development of the economic resources of Laos was confined mainly to the construction of a few trunk roads, one running parallel to the Mekong River and a few others leading into the interior. Most roads were useful for wheeled vehicles only during the dry season, and Laotians customarily measured distance by walking time.

The French Role in Cambodia

Under the imposition of a parallel French government for Cambodia, which the naval authorities at Saigon established in 1884, the Cambodian King was reduced to little more than the symbolic role as the embodiment of nationhood, religion, and authority. But his continued presence was, nevertheless, a potent and valuable political asset. For the villager, the royal palace continued to be the repository of divinely sanctioned authority, the magical center of the universe, and the abode of the god-king. The immaculate sacred sword was revered as the tool of Indra, and the counselling spirit which allegedly inhabited the seven-tiered parasol above the throne was still regarded as the source of both wisdom and power. Popular obedience to the King's commands was therefore automatic whenever these commands fell within the limits of traditional authority and were presumed to be dedicated to the national welfare and the promotion of the Buddhist religion. French officials operated behind this useful royal façade in carrying through essential administrative reforms. They encountered only one feeble armed protest when they assumed power in 1884.

But traditionalism had its serious disadvantages. The Buddhist monks who dominated the educational system, for example, viewed the country primarily as a depository of religious values and considered education as a special adjunct of religion. The French complained that pagoda schools did little more than encourage copying and memorization of Pali Buddhist texts while giving little or no attention to the actual reading and writing of the Cambodian language itself. Girls were left out of the traditional educational scheme entirely. But educational reform measures, which were introduced belatedly in 1918 for the purpose of correcting language training deficiencies, accomplished very little. Most villagers found literacy in Cambodian to be of little value. Students tended to drop out after the third grade, and promptly forgot what they had learned. The monks resisted French proposals to introduce a Romanized script and otherwise clung tenaciously to the Khmer tradition.

Other examples of resistance to change occurred in the economic field. Cambodia's rulers disliked the early French abolition of slavery, especially the cancellation of the obligations of debtor slaves. Slave service had traditionally constituted an important source of labor for public works and other royal projects. A semblance of compromise was eventually reached permitting the legal exaction of forced labor in the traditional French corvée pattern, a practice which continued down to 1948. Cambodians also demonstrated their traditional lack of interest in accumulating capital savings for investment and their reluctance to accept the regimentation of industrial employment. The country, economically, was accordingly limited to development within the French mercantilist pattern, except as a supplier and initial processor of basic commodities.

The only important French investment in the Cambodian economy was in rubber plantations, and these along with most of the processing plants were manned by Vietnamese labor. The timber concessions and saw mills, together with the rice mills, were run almost exclusively by Chinese entrepreneurs. Although many different mineral resources were known to be available in Cambodia, including phosphates, iron, coal, manganese, limestone, and salt, tentative plans made to develop them were abandoned by French groups in the face of local apathy and a lack of adequate transportation facilities. The positive role of the French government economically in Cambodia was confined for the most part to the licensing of such economic concessions as those for timber and fishing operations, to the collection of fees and taxes, and to the establishment of French language training schools for the elite population of the towns. The traditional ways of village life were tenaciously maintained, tied up as always with the observance of religious holidays, festival observances, and the annual rhythm of paddy cultivation and the fish harvest. Meanwhile, an abundance of undeveloped land and lack of population pressure prevented any serious economic unrest from developing.

Population growth in Cambodia was kept down by the prevalence of monasticism and by a continuing high death rate. The water supply was generally both quantitatively inadequate and cholera-contaminated. Proper sewage disposal was virtually nonexistent. Not until after World War I were any extensive efforts made to vaccinate for smallpox and cholera. A basic sanitary law was passed in 1930, but no facilities for health education were provided. The problem of drug addiction was less serious in Cambodia than among the Laotians because the use of opium was confined primarily to Chinese residents.

Cambodian attitudes toward alien elements of the population and neighboring peoples varied widely. Among the urban elite, including the professional and intellectual groups, French culture made a profound impression and was greatly admired. The Chinese population was also respected for its business success and admired as a group for being industrious, closely knit, and experienced, and for having much needed capital to invest. The Thai were regarded as "brothers," no doubt a little overbearing and presumptuous at times, but culturally akin. Laotians were treated by Cambodians as part of the same general family group, even though regarded as unsophisticated rustics. The Vietnamese were, by contrast, profoundly disliked by Cambodians as aliens, both culturally and ethnically. They had, since 1500, crowded the Khmers from the delta of the Mekong and were continuously infiltrating Cambodia's borders. French rule was acceptable in large measure because it protected Cambodians against Vietnamese domination and recovered for the Khmers border provinces claimed by Siam. The French rulers interfered little with the traditional tempo of Cambodian life, paid deference to the dignity of the Buddhist-supporting royal establishment, and restored many of the ancient monuments of Khmer greatness at Angkor, while at the same time maintaining peace and a moderate degree of prosperity. Cambodia was, therefore, the one area of French Indochina least likely to welcome the end of French rule.

Modernization in Siam, to 1910

The absence in Siam of direct alien political control contributed a distinctive quality to the modernizing process. This process was both pervasive and adaptable. Because the Court itself was the architect of the reforming program, the changes introduced did little to disrupt the traditional social order or to undermine governmental authority. The program avoided, therefore, the arousal of xenophobic rejection of alien influences *per se*, as happened in neighboring Burma. Village communities in Siam continued to be held together by kinship ties, by the authority of elected headmen, and by traditional popular allegiance to local chiefs or patrons. At the provincial level, the civil service officialdom functioned in the name of the King and also exercised authority in its own right as a professional bureaucracy. Siam's political agencies were not undermined in their status by subordination to an alien colonial authority, so that the government was not exposed to attacks from nationalistic political elements, which characterized other Southeast Asian countries after World Wars I and II. The royal Court continued to command popular reverence and unquestioned obedience in accordance with the age-old symbols of divine kingship. Even after the ruler lost his governing responsibilities in 1932, he played a continuing role as a traditional sanction to governmental authority.

Royally sponsored modernization worked fairly well during the reign of the able and respected King Chulalongkorn (Rama V, 1868-1910). His enlightened and liberal sentiments were demonstrated early in his reign. He abolished at the outset the required ceremonial prostration before the royal presence and initiated the gradual ending of slavery. He inaugurated in 1879 on a pilot basis a state-controlled system of secular education, and began granting stipends to several hundred state scholars, including royal princes, to be sent annually to Europe and to Japan for training. He established by royal edict the principle of religious toleration and set up a new advisory Privy Council. In the public building field, he constructed a new palace, which was furnished in European style, a postal-telegraph center, a museum, a hospital, an arsenal, and a dry dock. In the final decade of the century, the pace of modernization was stepped up, with the beginnings of railway construction and the installation of electric generators, telephone and telegraph facilities, and steamer service on the Menam River. Sunday was made a legal holiday, and press censorship was relaxed. In the area of health, a proper water supply system was provided for Bangkok, thus eliminating the perennial threat of cholera, and free vaccination was also introduced.

Traditional royal leadership as an instrument of modernization, nevertheless, carried with it serious limitations. Deference to divinely sanctioned kingly authority tended to inhibit all contrary views and placed a premium on official subservience rather than on efficient performance of duties. Prior to the crisis with France in 1892-93, Siam's foreign advisors were not permitted any real share in policy decisions, and even after enhancement of their role after that date, they exerted little real authority. By contrast, princely incumbents, who were frequently assigned to high-level government posts, usually treated their positions as lifetime sinecures, regardless of performance records. The wide gap between the divine ruler and his "slave" subjects simply could not be bridged. Most royal officials followed traditional patterns of moderate corruption and relaxed, lackadaisical administration. Officials in the provinces resisted reforming innovations, standards of justice long remained unimproved, and Bangkok itself was badly policed and governed.

The really remarkable aspect of Siam's modernization program was the loyal and effective service rendered by foreign advisers and a few of their princely associates, despite traditional impediments. German technicians supervised the establishment of the postal and telegraph systems and built the first railways. Danish officials and an Italian helped train the armed forces, including the officer corps. British advisers developed a land survey program, improved the system of revenue collections and disbursements, and undertook to extend popular education despite the lack of adequate funds. A Belgian assisted in conducting Siam's foreign affairs, and he was followed by several able Americans in the same role. A French lawyer supervised the reform of the legal code, which looked toward the eventual ending of extraterritoriality.

Much of the credit for administrative improvements after 1893 was the result of the leadership of Prince Damrong, a person of demonstrated organizing capacity and industry. He established the new Cabinet of Ministers to replace the traditional *Senabodi*, reorganized the local administrations under appointive, nonhereditary circle Commissioners (on the Burma model), and greatly improved financial administration. Although outside the capital of Bangkok Siam changed very slowly, the country governmentally and technologically was a very different place at the time of Chulalongkorn's death in 1910 than it had been in 1868.

A number of additional factors not connected with the inertia of tradition operated to retard Siam's economic development. Among them was the low rate of tax assessments on property and trade deriving from the nominal three to five per cent tax standards established for foreign-owned property under the 1855 treaties. Public revenues were simply not available for the accomplishment of needed improvements in such areas as roads, bunds, and irrigation channels.

The complete disappearance of slavery by 1905 denied the state a traditional source of labor service. No immigrant labor supply comparable to the Indian coolies used in Burma was available for Siam's economy. Most Chinese residents preferred to go into business activity or to work as artisans or as service personnel. Little risk capital, public or private, was available for economic expansion. French and British banks, established at Bangkok in the late eighties and the early nineties, were interested primarily in financing foreign trade. The British financial advisers to the government, furthermore, insisted on the maintenance of ample reserves in foreign currencies or bullion in order to facilitate foreign payment obligations. Credit needs of owner-cultivators were usually supplied sparingly by local patrons, a practice which slowed down agricultural expansion, but also accounted in part for the absence of land alienation as a problem. Actually, the expansion of rice production reached a plateau around 1893, after which date the surplus for export registered little increase for years. By 1900, Siam's foreign trade was falling behind Burma's in all important categories.

Siam gained from the limited nature of the colonial impact primarily in the preservation of her cultural and social integrity. In Siam there was no development of lawlessness among uprooted elements of the population, a situation which characterized Burma's rapidly expanding agricultural frontier. Traditional authority of local headmen, the bureaucracy, and the royal Court continued unimpaired, and Buddhist monks performed a constructive role. Continued identification of the Siamese state with the promotion of Buddhism involved no disruptive political and social implications, as happened in Burma. The importance of such differences was greatly magnified after World War II.

The modernization program in Siam began to encounter its first serious difficulties following the death of Chulalongkorn. His two sons, who succeeded him in turn, had been educated in Europe and were more or less alien in their tastes and point of view. This aspect of Siam's history, however, fits more properly into the post World War I period.

SEVEN

INTER-WAR DECADES AND WORLD WAR II

Divergent Trends

The period from the close of World War I to the end of World War II witnessed a growing divergence in the cultural and political development of the several Theravada Buddhist countries of Southeast Asia. French Laos changed very little except in the wider penetration of French cultural orientation among the upper and princely elite classes; economic and political changes were minimal. Cambodia also continued to function in accordance with pre-war cultural and administrative patterns, with the exception of an increasing incidence of overseas educational training for the social and political elites of the urban centers. Economic changes in Cambodia reflected in large measure the overflow influence of the heavy investments from metropolitan France in neighboring Cochin-China. These were channeled toward tea and rubber plantations, toward the improvement of transportation and water-control facilities associated with the growing volume of trade with the Saigon-Cholon port, and toward the modernization of Cambodia's capital city of Phnom Penh. Chinese and Vietnamese immigrants continued to penetrate Cambodia's borders in growing numbers, taking over much of the wholesale and retail trade and absorbing opportunities for industrial and plantation employment. The indigenous Khmer appeared to be generally satisfied with their little-disturbed status under the French protectorate, so that political agitation of a nationalist character was virtually nil. Even the novel experience of Japanese occupation during the course of the Far Eastern War, 1942-45, contributed very little to alter the situation in the two French-administered Buddhist territories, except as it paved the way for the eventual French withdrawal.

By contrast, the inter-war period witnessed in Siam and Burma very substantial changes, although quite different in character. During the 1920s Siam's government recovered its full sovereign status by renegotiating the unequal treaties contracted since 1855. This was accompanied by the development of nationalist sentiment. In 1932, a coterie of self-appointed modernist "promoters" drawn from the army command and from the European-educated political elite brought royal absolutism to an end. The new nationalist spirit was directed in part against the economic dominance of the resident Chinese population and, after 1939, toward the prospective recovery of lands lost to French and British colonial powers prior to World War I. Siam's new leadership endeavored in the late thirties and early forties to exploit the prospect of Japanese victory for the realization of nationalist ends.

Burma witnessed a resurgence of political and cultural nationalism of a radically different character. The situation was influenced during the inter-war decades by contemporaneous political developments in India and particularly by British efforts to meet Indian Congress demands for self-government. At the same time, the strong anti-Indian sentiment prevalent in Burma tended to balance off the unavoidable associations with the independence movement being staged in India. Burman nationalism was also greatly influenced by Buddhist religious partisanship and by superstitious survivals from the traditional kingship system. The educated elite were divided between those who, although nationalist, had something to lose from a complete disruption of the colonial system (civil servants, judges, lawyers, the European educated) and political partisans who had little stake in the existing pattern of affairs. A final faction was that of the students of the schools and Rangoon University, who despite their inexperience were destined to take over the political leadership after the war. The account of the inter-war period can best begin with a description of particular developments within Burma.

Burma and the Dyarchy System

The postwar opportunity held out in the declaration of 1917 by the Secretary of State for India, Lord Montagu, that postwar India would be accorded a larger measure of self-government, found Burmese nationalist sentiment inarticulate and poorly prepared to participate in the discussion. The only organized group available to react to the proposal was the Young Men Buddhist Association. It dated from the first decade of the century and counted a number of local chapters which usually met annually in the General Council of Buddhist Associations. It represented a tiny fraction of the population, its leadership being drawn from the younger elite. Its sponsors were concerned with the preservation of basic Buddhist aspects of

Burmese culture, but they lacked close connections with the traditionalist and, from their point of view, obscurantist Sangha monastic organization. One of the few successful efforts to establish rapport with majority Buddhist sentiment was made by the YMBA during the course of World War I when it raised the footwear-prohibition issue with respect to the use of pagoda premises. This issue was pressed more as a means of gaining face than as a matter of substantial importance; Burman Buddhists told their British rulers that they could not wear shoes while visiting pagoda premises, and the British residents in turn ignored the issue by ceasing to visit the pagoda premises where shoes were forbidden.

The leadership of this General Council of Buddhist Associations (GCBA) registered the only articulate reply to the decision of the Governor of Burma, made in late 1918, that Burma would not participate fully in the advance toward self-government contemplated by London for India proper. The issue of governmental reform, which had aroused little attention in Burma previously, quickly came alive when the suggestion was made that the county was not sufficiently advanced in political maturity and education to keep pace with India's progress.

From 1918 to 1922, the political pendulum went through a series of confusing gyrations. The initial demand of the GCBA spokesmen was for Burma's separation from India; then came their insistence, carried by a special delegation to London, that Burma not be excluded from the reforms. London finally decided in 1920 that Burma should participate in the emerging dyarchy system, which permitted several of the Ministries to be responsible to an elected Legislative Council. A long delay ensued, however, to determine what special adjustments would be necessary in the terms of the India Bill of 1919 if Burma were to be included.

During this interim period, from 1919 to 1922, application of the reforms in India proper ran afoul of nationalist resistance arising from the repressive Rowlatt Acts and the grim Amritsar Incident, where British-commanded troops shot down a large number of protesting civilians. By the time that the Burma Act was finally implemented, in 1922, the Gandhian boycott had been instituted in India, and most Burmans were no longer interested in participating in the Indian reforms. Under dyarchy as set up, half of the Ministers were made responsible to the elected Legislative Council. A politically motivated student strike at the newly established autonomous University of Rangoon dramatized increasing political tensions. The General Council of Buddhist Associations changed its name to

"Burmese Associations" and began to cultivate a wider political clientèle. Meanwhile, a generally successful effort was made to boycott elections scheduled under the reforms. Burmese nationalism thus got under way on an essentially negative pattern of reaction.

The discouraging story of the operation of dyarchy in Burma during the 1920s can be briefly summarized. In the three elections for the Legislative Council, held in 1922, 1925, and 1928, the percentage of the eligible voters who bothered to participate in the general constituency balloting ranged from seven per cent at the outset up to eighteen per cent in 1928. The boycotting element itself fragmented into a half-dozen political factions, and the 58 popularly elected members of the assembly divided into several more party groups. An additional 55 members of the Assembly represented communal constituencies and business groups or were direct appointees of the Governor. A working majority was maintained in the Council only by enticing one of the elected Burman factions plus particular individuals to cooperate with the variegated non-Burman minority elements. Controversial legislative proposals calculated to deal with urgent economic or administrative problems had to be studiously avoided to keep the artificial majority intact.

The country as a whole seemed to care very little about what went on in the Assembly. At the grass roots village level, political agitation centered around repeal of certain householder taxes and the fanning of the fires of religious partisanship. The most extreme faction of the boycotting political elements was led by a political-minded monk named U Ottama, who returned to Burma from India in 1921. He had previously been a student at the University of Calcutta and had also visited Japan. His spirited allegation that Buddhism was in danger at the hands of an alien and oppressive government found a response in the organization of numerous village *athin* nationalist cells. He was twice imprisoned for treasonable utterances during the course of the decade, became hopelessly demented during the early thirties, and eventually died in prison. Another monk who also died as an alleged martyr to the cause was U Wisara. He staged a fatal hunger strike in prison rather than surrender his yellow robe. Although such political agitation was usually frowned upon by the truly pious members of the Sangha, who took seriously their presumed nonconcern with mundane affairs, the activities of the political pongyis continued to attract wide attention throughout the countryside. Political agitation tended in time to coalesce with ordinary lawlessness in many situations where the authority of the village headman was flouted. Some monastery precincts in urban areas became depositories for stolen property. Sincere Buddhists who deplored the increasing demoralization of the monkhood in the atmosphere of growing political tension nevertheless sympathized with the nationalist goals of the rabble rousers, even though overt extremism was deplored.

Burmese political obscurantism found its final expression in the Saya San Rebellion of 1930-31. Saya San was a practitioner of Burmese medicines, the author of a book on the subject, an *ex-pongyi*, and a one-time leader of a radical faction of the GCBA. His activities centered in the traditionally restive Lower Burma province of Tharrawaddy, where he gained a considerable following. He constructed a crude palace in the jungle, replete with all of the traditional symbols of divine kingship. His followers tatooed themselves to attain invulnerability to firearms, manufactured crude weapons from pipe and bicycle tubing, and murdered a British government officer in order to enlist the aid of his spirit in their mad venture of rebellion. The effort was utterly fanatical and had to be put down with considerable bloodshed. Saya San was captured, brought to trial under a Burmese judge, convicted, and sentenced to death.

Meanwhile, a visiting Commission was reviewing the operation of the dyarchy system in preparation for the next stage of self-government to be worked out by a scrics of Indian and Burman Roundtable Conferences in London. Dyarchy in Burma had been something short of a signal achievement as a constitutional experiment. The circle boards and district councils elected to represent the villager in the exercise of local government had been even less successful than was the central Legislative Council. The local councils had been entrusted with responsibilities beyond their competence and were susceptible to all manner of corruption. And yet the Simon Commission had no choice but to recommend an extension of self-rule and the separation of Burma from India. The Commission was apparently unaware of the widespread popular distrust of London's intentions.

The Burma Constitution of 1935

The efforts of the British government to consult with representative Burmese spokesmen at successive Roundtable Conferences in 1930-31 concerning the nature of the revised constitution eventually ran aground in a morass of distrust and misunderstanding. Most informed Burmans favored separation from India as an essential step in the establishment of national identity and in the escape from Indian economic domination. Propaganda emanating from nationalist quarters in India, however, advanced the theory that the British, in an alleged divide-and-rule tactic, intended to give Burma inferior treatment. The Burmese, therefore, had better go along with India. Such suspicions of British intentions found ready acceptance in village *athins*, which were influenced by the *pongyis* and the boycotting GCBA. British residents within Burma, who were traditionally hostile to greater self-rule, were so unanimously in favor of separation that Burman fears were seemingly confirmed, and official British spokesmen at the London Roundtable Conferences did nothing to dispel such distrust. An election held in 1932, in which the boycott was abandoned, registered a resounding victory for the anti-separationists, who also rejected London's only alternative proposal of Burma's permanent association with India. Partisan excitement stifled all efforts at judicious consideration. In the end the British Parliament ignored the election mandate and drew up a separate constitution for Burma, which was in fact fully as liberal in character as that given to India. The full Cabinet was made responsible to the fully elected Assembly, and half of the Senate was elected by the lower House. The Governor retained emergency executive powers in addition to veto power authority over legislation.

Before this new Constitution of 1935 was put into operation in 1937, the important Student Strike of 1936 occurred at the University of Rangoon. It was precipitated and exploited by a small fraction of the students referring to themselves as "Thakins" (masters) and connected with the *Dobama Asiayone* (We Burmans Association), a radical nationalist organization. Led by Thakins Nu, Aung San, Kyaw Nyein, and Ba Swe, this group captured control of the Rangoon University Student Union during the fall session of 1935. Student grievances were not lacking, and the strike developed in February, 1936, on the eve of the final yearly examinations, which were for many an awesome ordeal. But the motivation for the strike was essentially anti-colonial in character and emphasis. All approaches to examination halls were blocked by the prostrate forms of the strikers, and the exams had to be postponed. From the University, the strike spread to the high schools throughout the province, thus commanding the attention of virtually the entire literate population. The strikers received solicitous attention from nationalist politicians seeking to make capital from such activities, and they were accorded support from the public generally. The Thakin sponsors of the strike were destined to become leading champions of Burmese nationalism, first in opposition to the British and later in opposition to the Japanese.

The immediate achievements of the strike were minimal. The postponed examinations were held in June instead of March, and some political representation was added to the governing board of the University. The older politicians did not take the Thakins very seriously, especially after the participation of the *Dobama Asiayone* in the elections of 1936 produced only three members of the new Legislative Assembly. But the Thakins and others participating in the strike experience represented a dedicated and uncompromising nationalist leadership not amenable to office or bribe offers, as many of the older politicos tended to be. Nor were the student-nationalists beholden to the obscurantist leadership of the U Ottamas or the Saya Sans. They eventually became associated with the so-called "Freedom Bloc" organized by ex-Premier Ba Maw, and many of them, including Thakin Nu, suffered imprisonment for subversive utterances following the outbreak of the war in Europe. The Thakin group's "thirty heroes" fled the country and returned with the invading Japanese in 1942. This student fraction of the nationalist movement of the nineteen thirties provided virtually all of the top political leadership of the reborn Burmese nation following the war. Unfortunately, two of the ablest leaders, Aung San and Thakin Mya, suffered assassination in 1947.

Burma Under the Revised Constitution, 1937-41

The first elections under the revised constitution of 1935, held in 1936, were inconclusive in their results. The victorious Independent party contained so many fragmented elements that its cohesion gave way when the political rewards proved to be insufficient to satisfy all elements of the coalition. As a result, the first Cabinet was organized by the clever European-trained lawyer, Dr. Ba Maw, drawn from his personal following plus the medley of communal and minority elements, including even the British contingent within the Legislative Assembly. Although Christian-trained, Dr. Ba Maw was bitterly Anglophobe, having abandoned Oxford in favor of Bordeaux to obtain his advanced degree in law. He first gained political prominence by volunteering as defense counsel for the trial of Saya San, and had later become one of the more articulate advocates of the anti-separationist point of view. His own Sinyetha (poor man's) party had made a poor showing in the election, partly because its socialist-type platform was poorly understood. Ba Maw managed for two years to maintain a heterogeneous majority by holding in abeyance his vaguely socialistic principles.

Dr. Ba Maw's government was subjected to virulent challenge

both within and outside the Legislative Assembly, but it did move forward. His government sponsored the preparation of a series of able reports covering such basic problems as tenancy, land alienation, and agricultural financing. Little in the way of tangible reform was accomplished during his short two years' tenure, but preliminary steps were taken for the passage in 1939 of a Tenancy Act intended to end the evil practice of annual leases and of a Land Purchase Act, hopefully designed to facilitate the recovery of titles by cultivators. Both of the reforms encountered serious difficulties in implementation. Other studies were instituted for the purpose of halting land alienation and of providing more generous agricultural financing, but they were sidetracked by a conservative-minded Senate and by the intrusion of more urgent political considerations connected with the outbreak of the European part of World War II. In mid-1938 Premier Ba Maw's political opponents, led by fanatical *pongyi* agitators, instigated a round of anti-Indian riots, which were followed by industrial strikes and student demonstrations. Such problems led to the disintegration of his Legislative majority in early 1939.

U Pu took over after Dr. Ba Maw. His premiership was characterized by attempts to democratize the office of village headman, by authorization of a searching exposé of bribery and corruption prevailing at the lower and middle levels of governmental administration, and by repercussions connected with political events in India, Europe, and Eastern Asia. The real power behind the government of Premier U Pu was a lawyer-politician and newspaper editor named U Saw, who had been largely instrumental in instigating the 1938 riots. U Saw bided his time under U Pu's leadership for a year and a half. Then in September 1940, he defected from the government and took over power in his own right.

The outbreak of the European war in 1939 prompted the formation of a so-called "Freedom Bloc" led by the ousted Dr. Ba Maw, which also included prominent members of the Thakin nationalists. The group demanded as a condition of Burma's cooperation in the war effort that Britain recognize Burma's right to independence, make preparations for a constituent assembly, and concede Cabinet control over the powers reserved to the Governor in the Constitution of 1935—powers which covered foreign policy, constitutional changes, finances, and administration of peripheral non-Burman sections of the country. Ba Maw, Thakin Nu, and other spokesmen of the Freedom Bloc were subsequently imprisoned for treasonable utterances. U Pu was thrown sharply on the defensive when he refused to subscribe to Freedom Bloc demands and pledged instead in mid-1940 unqualified support of Britain's war effort against Nazi Germany. The resulting situation afforded opportunity for U Saw's defection.

The wily U Saw was as willing as U Pu to give formal assurances of support for the British war effort, but he also exploited the situation unrelentingly for his personal political profit. His vigorous efforts to curb press criticism and to suppress internal unrest afforded him opportunity to put down all of his political rivals as well as all subversive elements. He solicited nationalist support by championing such popular causes as the Burmanization of the civil service (ostensibly in the interest of economy), free primary education, a Buddhist university, and the discontinuance of English as the medium of instruction at the University of Rangoon. In October 1940, he reopened the Burma Road for the transportation of military supplies to China and discontinued publishing pro-Japanese propaganda in his own newspaper. When the Far Eastern war actually broke in December 1941, U Saw was on his way back to Burma from England, via the United States, after having attempted unsuccessfully to extract a pledge from Winston Churchill of postwar independence for his country. Retracing his journey via Europe, the Premier was detected in Lisbon engaging in treasonable communication with the Japanese legation. He was accordingly arrested in Egypt and imprisoned for the duration in British Uganda. During the short interim period prior to the complete Japanese conquest of Burma, Governor Sir Reginald Dorman-Smith rounded up a conservative Burman Cabinet which later followed him to Simla, India, to serve as the wartime government in exile.

Siam, 1910 to 1932

Dynastic leadership in Siam's program of modernization reached a point of diminishing returns following the death of King Chulalongkorn in 1910. The two sons who in turn succeeded him had been educated in Europe and were too alien in their interests and orientation to fit constructively into the governmental affairs of Bangkok. Reforms achieved after 1910, owed little to royal initiative. By the early 1930s, the sacrosanct status of the ruler had been so eroded that restive elements of the army and the nonroyal elite openly challenged princely nepotism and the consequent lack of vigor and imagination within the government. In the noncolonial atmosphere of Siam, traditionalist obscurantism, as exemplified in the pongyi politicians and the Saya Sans of Burma, did not emerge as an impediment to the modernization program.

The bizarre interests and confused policies of Rama VI (1910-25) did much to discredit capricious absolutism. As a dilettante dramatist and actor, Rama VI was decidedly uninterested in routine affairs of state. He was extravagant in his expenditures from the royal purse, and he made no effort to curb corruption and inefficiency in the administration. A group of youthful flatterers gained his ear to the exclusion of official councilors of greater wisdom and experience. His personal bodyguard was provided fancy uniforms, a clubhouse, and a rugby football team. Army cliques staged two abortive plots during his reign. Rama VI ostensibly favored a Buddhist revival along with a continuation of untrammelled absolutism, but he championed at the same time a program of compulsory secular primary education which was counter to tradition. Except for the elimination of German experts during and after World War I, he continued to use foreign advisers at virtually all levels and categories of the Siamese administration.

The younger brother, Rama VII (1925-35) was more liberally inclined, but he succeeded in offending almost everyone and proved entirely unable to implement ill-defined reform proposals. Although ostensibly he favored constitutional government and parliamentary procedures, he permitted princely incumbents opposed to such views to monopolize the High Council of the government. Princely bureaucrats, for example, were exempted from the application of the Civil Service Law of 1928. At the same time, he failed completely to promote popular understanding of the alleged advantages of representative government or to enlist elite support for his proposed reforms. The nobility was particularly offended by his abolition of the Department of Royal Pages, which had customarily trained their sons. The army bureaucratic leadership resented unavoidable economies affecting the public services which were imposed during the depression years of 1930-32.

The one notable accomplishment of the reign of Rama VII, the renegotiation of the unequal treaties of the nineteenth century, owed very little to the King himself. This was primarily the work of Francis B. Sayre, the son-in-law of President Wilson, who served from 1920 to 1927 as Siam's Foreign Office adviser. Prior to World War I, only a few minor relaxations of the extraterritorial privileges accorded European subjects residing in Siam had been achieved. The original treaties of the 1850s had provided no time limit after which revision could be sought, and modification could, therefore, be achieved only by mutual consent. President Wilson responded affirmatively to Bangkok's plea made at the Versailles Peace Conference by renegotiating the American treaty in 1920. American residents thereafter could be tried under Siamese law. The previous fiscal and tariff restrictions were also lifted, and the new treaty was itself made terminable after ten years on application of either party. Sayre's assigned task was to obtain general acceptance of the revisions agreed to by President Wilson. Progress at first was slow. A suitable Japanese treaty was arranged in 1924, but negotiations with the French and the British ran aground for some time thereafter.

Siam's final escape from the limitations of her unequal treaties came in part as a result of the victory of the Kuomintang Nationalists in China in 1925-26. European reservations against treaty reform based on the need for a new legal code, their continued interest in trade privileges and boundary considerations receded in importance after 1925. It became apparent that the new Nanking regime, the first Chinese regime to be interested in overseas residents, would surely raise the issue of negotiating a consular treaty with Bangkok to extend extraterritorial jurisdiction over the three million or so Chinese living in Siam who were still claimed as citizens of China under the *ius sanguinis* rule. The French concession of a new consular treaty made in 1925 was accompanied by a frontier settlement establishing a demilitarized zone on both sides of the Mekong River boundary plus the enjoyment of reciprocal rights by Siamese citizens resident in French Indochina equal to those accorded to French nationals in Siam. The British negotiated a similar treaty shortly thereafter which specified the continuance for ten years of a moderate tariff (set at five per cent) on cotton yarn, textiles, iron and steel products, and machinery. Other treaty powers followed suit. By the end of the 1930s, all vestiges of the unequal treaty privileges were swept away. Francis Sayre was generously honored for his valuable services by the Siamese government.

During the latter half of the 1920s, the Siamese nationalists also attempted to curb the extensive economic influence of the Chinese residents. The added importance attached to national identity on both sides was intensified by the militant spirit of China's new Kuomintang regime and by the increasing immigration into Siam of Chinese women. This latter development reduced the rate of assimilation and the degree of transiency of Siam's largest alien community. Previous legal advantages enjoyed by the Chinese in owing no personal service to the King and in being asked to pay fewer types of taxes were arbitrarily cancelled by 1930. Communal friction increased after the revolution of 1932, when many Chinese schools were closed. Vocational opportunities for non-Siamese citizens were also restricted, and immigration was reduced to an approximate 10,000 a year.

The Revolutionary Bangkok Regime, 1932-41

The revolutionary "promoters" who took over control of the Siamese government from the King in July 1932 did so in the name of progress and reform. Acting partly from conviction and partly to provide an attractive façade to ward off possible British or French intervention on behalf of the friendly royalist faction, the new leaders championed a number of far-reaching liberal changes. They proposed to establish a constitution, freedom of the press, social equality and popular education, substitution of a graduated income tax for the unpopular land tax assessments, and establishment of a genuinely competitive civil service. Rama VII apparently had himself lost faith in the monarchial system, and he refused at the outset to use the police power available to him to suppress the activities of the army-backed promoters of the revolution. He returned to Europe for medical reasons in early 1934, thus sacrificing any chance of re-establishing royal control. His eventual denunciation of the regime in 1935 as militaristic and undemocratic was the prelude to his abdication. The successor chosen by the government was a ten-year-old nephew who was at the time at school in Switzerland. The role of the Siamese monarchy was thus reduced to that of a symbol only, although its popularity among the Siamese people has remained surprisingly unimpaired throughout succeeding decades.

Faced with conditions of economic depression, the new regime, led initially by the French-trained Leftist Law Academy Professor, Pridi Phanamyong, formulated a new progressive pattern for Siamese development. Pridi's program called for a planned economy conforming in some respects to the Soviet system. Proposed governmental operation of major industrial and commercial activities would serve allegedly not only to end the Chinese economic stranglehold, but also to lay the foundation for expanded productivity and employment and for better labor-employer relations. The government would supply the needed capital and marketing facilities. The issuance of state bonds would provide funds for the purchase of land for redistribution to cultivator-tenants, a reform to be accompanied by other educational and welfare measures. Pridi Phanamyong suggested originally that all political authority be vested in a Peoples party, from which alone could be drawn the candidates for election to the Assembly. Pridi's Leftist proposals found little support outside his coterie of personal followers, but they clearly reflected the prevailing lack of confidence in any genuinely democratic scheme of government and the attractiveness of a state-directed approach.

Siam's first constitution, drawn up in late 1932 and continuing in force until 1946, was fashioned from the political realities of the immediate situation. It preserved some of the prestige of the royal Court by reserving for the royal prerogative decision on several minor items. It nevertheless excluded the princes from membership in the Cabinet and the new State Council, provided for the election by indirect suffrage of half of the Legislative Assembly, and assigned to the ruling party leadership the appointment of the other half of the Assembly. The Cabinet would be responsible to a majority of the Assembly, but the budget from the previous year could be applied in emergency situations. Lacking was any articulate popular demand for political participation or any genuine public interest in the character of the Assembly. Elected provincial representatives to the Assembly developed in time a vested interest in sharing some of the perquisites of political power with the ruling Bangkok clique. The authority of the government at the village level owed much to continuing popular respect for the role of the official bureaucracy and for the aura of divine kingship. The new regime was thoroughly indigenous in both its capacities and shortcomings.

Because the army was the best-organized fragment of the new political structure, control gravitated during 1933 into conservative military hands. Rightist elements forced Pridi into temporary exile and outlawed Communism. A half-hearted royalist coup was put down later in the same year. The able Pridi was allowed to return to the Cabinet in 1934 to serve successively as Minister of the Interior, of Foreign Affairs, and of Finance. He continued to be the idol of the youthful intelligentsia, but was obliged after 1937 to share the spotlight with Colonel Luang Pibun Songgram. Their rivalry persisted for a full decade thereafter. The retirement of the titular Premier Phaya Bahol in 1938 because of ill health permitted executive leadership to gravitate toward Colonel Pibun, who was backed at the time by the conservative Assembly which had been selected in the previous year. Pridi and other civilians remained in the Cabinet for a time, but ambitious army elements exercised actual control.

In addition to the curbing of princely power, an essential feature of nationalistic policy at Bangkok during the latter half of the thirties was its anti-Chinese character. The unpopular land and capitation taxes were repealed in favor of a one per cent income levy and a two per cent tax on Chinese-dominated trade. Principal sources of revenue continued to be from opium sales, customs and excise levies, and fees and licenses on shops, banking operations, and amusements, in all of which activities the Chinese were heavily involved. Some twenty-five professions were legally designated as reserved for the Siamese population, and the use of the Chinese language in school instruction was forbidden. Anti-Chinese measures proliferated as Japanese influence in Eastern Asia mounted following Tokyo's full-scale attack on China after 1937. Nationalism in Siam, as contrasted with anti-colonialism in Burma, was positively pro-Thai. It combined the principle of single-party rule with effective army control. It later exploited Japanese support in order to recover irredentist territories in the Mekong valley and on the Cambodian borders which had been lost to France during the score of years prior to World War I. Military expenditures were sharply increased by Pibun after 1937, and the use of Western advisers was drastically cut back.

Another principal trend in Siam was that of increased governmental participation in trade and manufacturing ventures. The pattern of official operation of such public services as railways, telegraphs, and electrical generating plants had already been set by European advisers. The new government expanded its operations to include paper and textile factories, sugar and tobacco processing plants, silk establishments, and oil refineries. Most of these ventures operated at a chronic loss because of inefficient management and official corruption. Rubber production, however, made noteworthy gains after 1934. It was, nevertheless, a debatable question whether Siam's new modernizing regime during the seven years prior to the outbreak of the European war demonstrated marked improvement over royal leadership.

Following the outbreak of war, Premier Pibun assumed a frankly jingoist militarist pose. Siamese race and culture, including the Buddhist faith, became for him objects of patriotic veneration. The country's name was changed officially from Siam to Thailand, and a Pan-Thai movement of indefinite dimensions was launched. It comprehended, theoretically, territories in Malaya as far south as Kedah and Penang, all of Burma's Tenasserim coast and the easternmost Shan states, plus regions taken over by France since 1893. One-third of the national revenue was allocated to military preparations. Pibun's pro-Japanese orientation included the fashioning of a Thai version of the *bushido* ethic of the samurai, the acceptance of Japanese "mediation" in the 1941 dispute with France over the Laotian border in the Mekong valley, and a general acquiescence in Tokyo's claim that Japan shared Thai reverence for the Buddhist faith. Japan set up a full embassy at Bangkok in 1940, as well as two consulates at Singora on the borders of Malaya and at Chiengmai near the border of Burma's Kengtung State. Presumably the logic of events, a "bending to the wind," rather than any overt decision produced Pibun's wartime alignment with the Japanese aggression. Also bearing on the situation was Thailand's noncolonial status which enabled Bangkok to attempt a peaceful adjustment to the threatened dominance of Southeast Asia by Japan, thus sparing the country dire military effects experienced elsewhere.

Effects of the Japanese Occupation

The effects of the Japanese intrusion into Buddhist Southeast Asia during the Far Eastern war of 1941-45 were highly disparate even though the discrediting of European prestige and the stimulation of indigenous nationalist sentiment were generally prevalent. All of French Indochina was occupied following the fall of France in the summer of 1940. The Vichy regime of Marshal Petain ordered the surrender under pressure from Germany, and the local French authorities were powerless to counter Japanese control. Cochin-China became the staging point for the Japanese land forces which overran continental Southeast Asia in early 1942, and Cambodia was the corridor for invasion of Siam. Laos escaped with little interference from the Japanese partly because it produced nothing that the invaders needed and partly because it lay across no useful avenue of communication leading to Burma or into South China. Until the early spring of 1945, the Japanese left the conduct of routine governmental functions in Indochina to the local French authorities, although the conquerors assumed control over all transportation facilities and seized whatever supplies were required by the military.

French officialdom, on the whole, staged a stubborn retreat and managed to preserve a measure of prestige, especially in Laos and Cambodia. This was the result in considerable measure of local resentment in Laos and Cambodia over Thailand's endeavors, with Japanese help, to recover border regions incorporated into Indochina after 1893. The elite groups in Cambodia, in Champassak province of southern Laos, and at the royal Court at Luang Prabang were thus still pro-French at the end of the war. The returning French forces had little difficulty in re-establishing control throughout the Mekong valley in late 1945. Thailand was in 1945 itself more virulently anti-French than either of its neighbors to the east, and Bangkok therefore became the rendezvous for such disgruntled elements as the Lao Issara faction mentioned in Chapter One.

As previously indicated, Thailand after 1938 followed its traditional policy of aligning itself with what appeared to be the winning side, especially so under the government of Pibun Songgram. Negotiations with Western powers during the prewar years for possible military protection enlisted little positive response except from the United States, and that prospect was later to be destroyed by Pearl Harbor and the Japanese invasion of the Philippines. Japanese aid was accepted in Siam's recovery of border Indochina areas in 1941; later accretions of territory in Malaya and along Burma's Shan States border occurred in 1942. Four Malay sultanates were acquired, two Shan states, and two Cambodian provinces. The Japanese assumed control over all railway and airport facilities in Thailand. The invaders also flooded the country with billions of paper yen matched by no consumer imports, so that a ten-to-one inflation of prices ensued, coupled with an orgy of official corruption. But the countryside was not devastated nor was the population despoiled, except for victimized Chinese elements identified as friendly to Nationalist China. The Bangkok government itself was only moderately less anti-Chinese than Japan. Pibun obediently declared war on both the United States and Britain and committed his regime in pretty thoroughgoing fashion to a Japanese victory. The Thai authorities assumed responsibility for the internment of enemy aliens overtaken by the events of the war. The major invasion thrusts of the Japanese forces against both Malaya and Burma were staged via Thailand.

Burma by comparison suffered from the full brunt of the Japanese military offensive and also from the denial measures taken by the British-Indian forces. The Japanese entered by the Tenasserim corridor far more speedily and in greater numbers than had been anticipated. They enjoyed some useful assistance from Burman collaborators headed by Thakins Soe, Aung San, Ne Win, and others of the "thirty heroes" who had fled from Burma during U Saw's regime. The tactic of infiltration to the rear of established British defenses was effectively employed by the invaders, and the early collapse of the lower Sittang River defense line forced the abandonment of the capital and port of Rangoon in early March of 1942. The difficult retreat of British forces northward up the Irrawaddy River valley was complicated by supply problems, by the blistering sun of the hot season, the eventual lack of air cover, and by the encumbering presence of tens of thousands of Indian refugees. A Chinese army commanded by General Joseph Stilwell of the United States effectively defended for a time the Sittang valley corridor, but it gave way when threatened in the rear by Japanese forces penetrating the Karenni state and the Shan plateau regions to the east and north. Burman collaborators, including recruits from the political *pongyis*, proved to be almost as much an embarrassment as an aid to the Japanese, while the population as a whole took no part in the harrowing campaign.

Initial efforts of the youthful Thakins to impose a substitute civilian regime to take the place of the retreating British authorities miscarried badly, and the Japanese in the late spring nominated ex-Premier Dr. Ba Maw to head a puppet regime. He was assisted by personal followers and by selected leadership from Thakin circles. As *Adipati* (Chief of State), Ba Maw did what he could short of precipitating a complete break with his Japanese masters, to protect his people from mistreatment. He insisted that the Shan States area be conceded to be Burmese. He assembled thirty thousand laborers to work on Japanese projects, including the "railway of death" from Moulmein into Thailand, and otherwise committed himself so fully to a Japanese victory as to ruin his future career as a Burmese politician. He also demonstrated his personal vanity and ambition by assuming the aura of kingship with the title of *Mingyi*, while venting his contempt for democratic institutions. He conducted himself creditably at the end of the war by refusing to divulge to the military authorities the plans to turn against the Japanese developed by his Thakin associates in the government.

The sufferings of the Burmese people under the Japanese occupation were dire. What little was left of transportation facilities following the British-Indian withdrawal was monopolized exclusively for the military needs of the invaders. Cattle were requisitioned for purposes of food and transportation, and like Thailand the country was flooded with printed currency. Rice surpluses in Lower Burma could neither be exported nor shipped upcountry where a shortage of food developed. The products of Upper Burma, including cooking oils and cotton, were similarly denied transportation to the delta regions. The Japanese soldiery treated Burmese elders with contempt, violated sacred pagoda precincts, and showed no respect for the yellow-robed *pongyis*. The Kempeitai, or military police, in particular was guilty of callous brutality. More than two million acres of paddy land reverted to jungle during the course of the war, and virtually no consumer goods imports were introduced to match the newly printed currency.

When the Japanese realized in early 1943 that Burma would have to be used as a major base of military operations either for the invasion of India or for defense against Allied counterattack, some measure of autonomy was accorded to Dr. Ba Maw's regime. An independence Preparatory Committee drafted a constitution during the first half of the year, and the "independence" of Burma was duly celebrated in August, 1943. The Cabinet consisted of personal followers of the *Adipati* plus a selection from the Thakin group headed by Aung San, but it enjoyed little authority except in those areas of government completely divorced from military needs and control. Dr. Ba Maw followed the example of Pibun Songgram by declaring war on the United States and Great Britain. He also collaborated with the head of the Japanese-sponsored Indian National Army, Subhas Chandra Bose of Bengal, in making preparations for the invasion of India, which was attempted in 1944. Meanwhile, his Thakin associates within the government developed secret connections with associates in India and with underground anti-Japanese elements, perfecting their plans to turn on the thoroughly hated Japanese once the opportunity arose.

Burma's Liberation

Although General Joseph Stilwell, the Deputy Allied Commander to Lord Louis Mountbatten, became very impatient over the British delay in launching a sustained overland counteroffensive against the Japanese in Burma, the British plan was no doubt the sounder approach. Lord Mountbatten preferred to assemble the necessary resources and manpower in India, including large army contingents from British Africa, and then wait for the Japanese to overreach themselves. The opportunity came at the opening of the rainy season in June, 1944, when the Japanese effort to invade India ran aground in Manipur and Assam and their logistic services via Burma broke down. The counterattacking British-Indian and African troops had to contend with the same rains, but they had the advantage of the air support for supply purposes which operated from American bases in the Assam and Calcutta areas. The simultaneous Japanese attack launched in early 1944 along the Arakan-Chittagong coastal region ran aground partly because of terrain difficulties and partly because the Indian National Army contingents, headed by Subhas Bose, proved entirely useless in their efforts to subvert the opposition when faced with African instead of Indian troops. The Japanese retreat developed into a rout, and no effective counterstand was made until the central Burma plain was reached in early 1945.

During the final stages of the Burma campaign, the Japanese offered determined resistance to the efforts of Allied forces to reach the principal port of Rangoon. This goal had to be accomplished before the return of the monsoon season in late May, as the rains would disrupt land supply routes from India in the same fashion that the Japanese themselves had experienced in the previous year. Failure to capture Rangoon would have made necessary a difficult seaborne attack against the Irrawaddy delta, for which the necessary equipment was simply not available. It was in this military context that the proffered assistance of Thakin Aung San and the Anti-Fascist League army to strike the Japanese of Lower Burma in the rear was accepted by Lord Louis Mountbatten, much to the distress of London and Burma's Governor Sir Reginald Dorman-Smith at Simla. Mountbatten's decision was important politically for the future of Burma, for it gave to Aung San and his nationalist associates the status of *de facto* allies to the returning British armies and the chance, once victory had been achieved, to come into the open to recruit a more representative following from all elements of articulate nationalist leadership of the country. Militarily, Mountbatten's policies paid off well. After March 28, 1945, when the Burmese struck at the Japanese rear, the British advance southward increased from the rate of a few miles to around 30 miles per day. The Japanese made their final hopeless stand near Pegu north of Rangoon on May 1, and then withdrew in the direction of Thailand along the same routes by which they had invaded Burma more than three years before.

Lord Mountbatten's determination to preserve good relations with the Burman nationalist leadership centering in the Anti-Fascist Peoples Freedom League was defended on the grounds that Burma must provide a dependable Allied base for mounting further operations to liberate the remainder of Southeast Asia. It was actually two full months after the surrender of the Japanese in Tokyo in August that the civilian authorities led by Governor Dorman-Smith returned to Rangoon. It then proved too late to counter the almost universal popularity of Thakin Aung San and his nationalist associates. The British returned U Saw from Uganda and Dr. Ba Maw from Japan, whence he had fled, in order to provide possible political counter-attractions to Aung San. The sustained efforts of the Governor and his conservative and more senior Burmese supporters to recover control were to no avail.

The Attlee Government in London vetoed, in April 1946, Dorman-Smith's provocative proposal to arrest Aung San on criminal charges, and a replacement in the person of Sir Hubert Rance drawn from Mountbatten's previous staff was selected to take over the Governorship. Governor Rance arrived in late August, barely in time to avert open rebellion. Aung San and associates were promptly admitted to the Cabinet, and they were later invited to London in early 1947 to work out the details of the independence program. The Burmese themselves in the spring elected a Consituent Assembly which drafted a proposed constitution later ratified by London. The country thus assumed its complete independence in January 1948.

The smooth and generously conceived program of transition to independence was marred by the tragic murder in July 1947 of the two ablest of the youthful nationalist leaders, Thakin Aung San and Thakin Mya. U Saw was the perpetrator of the deed, apparently conceived in the hope that he could blame it on the British and would be able himself to seize control during the ensuing period of confusion. Governor Rance selected Thakin Nu, Aung San's close friend since their student days, to take over control, and a political crisis was thus averted. As the first Premier of the new Burma Union which commenced in January 1948, Nu managed to curb the multiple rebellions which tortured Burma during the first several years following independence, but he proved ineffective as an administrator. The ablest of the older trained politicians and civil servants from British times were either ignored as with Dr. Ba Maw, or eliminated by assassination, as with U Tin Tut, leaving the topmost posts manned by inexperienced persons who eventually divided into rival factions. Local officials, meanwhile, were demoralized by the impact of rebellion and political interference.

The other major handicap which independent Burma suffered as compared with its Buddhist neighbors derived from the wholesale material destruction which it endured during the course of two extended military campaigns. Its railways were largely destroyed, its river steamers were sunk, its highway bridges were out, and its principal port facilities and public services were left in ruins. Paddy lands reverted to jungle and long proved incapable of redevelopment amid the chronic disorders, while the financial and administrative structure of the fledgling state fell into complete disarray. Urban areas became crowded by squatter refugees.

Summary of Postwar Situations: Cambodia

As the Buddhist states of Southeast Asia emerged from the ordeal of the Japanese occupation into the postcolonial era, they faced sharply differing situations. The astute King Norodom Sihanouk of Cambodia obtained, without any overt struggle against the French, full recognition of his country's independence and the recovery of the border provinces taken over in 1941-42 by Thailand. Recognizing that growing political agitation emanating from ultra-nationalist and Communist sources would have to be countered with vigor, the prince resigned his kingship in favor of a relative and entered the contest as an active political leader. Taking full advantage of his princely status and his personal attractiveness in both physical appearance and personality, he rode the wave of a reviving sense of Cambodian nationalism. He made a special effort to enlist the services of the youthful educated elite.

When United States concern over Communist threats to Laos, Thailand, and South Vietnam prompted the formation of the SEATO alliance and the granting of substantial gifts of military supplies to Cambodia's traditionally enemy neighbors, Prince Norodom elected to follow a different course. He relegated considerations of the cold war to a secondary level as compared with the assumed threat of extinction which his country faced from the pressure of immediate neighbors. He also began deliberate efforts to seek an accommodation with Communist China and North Vietnam on both political and ideological grounds. He calculated that China would be around in Eastern Asia long after the United States had lost interest in Cambodia, and he strongly discounted the wisdom and effectiveness of the strident American anti-Communist program staged in both Laos and South Vietnam. The combination of the aura of divine royalty and a rising sense of national pride, coupled with the amalgam of popular hatred and fear of distrusted neighbors virtually eliminated serious domestic disaffection within Cambodia. Prince Norodom's acceptance of economic assistance from both Communist and American sources was cleverly executed and tended to improve the economic outlook.

Laos

The postwar situation in Laos differed from that of Cambodia in that the successive titular rulers at Luang Prabang lost any vestige of political initiative, leaving the contest for postwar power to be waged between princely descendants of the vice-regal line. One of these, Prince Boun Oum of Champassak, together with his youthful protégé General Phoumi Nosavan, was pro-French in sympathy following the conclusion of the war. Two others, Souphanouvong and Petsarath, were decidedly anti-French and also opposed to the royal leadership at Luang Prabang. Souphanouvong eventually accepted assistance from the anti-French Viet Minh rebels of Vietnam. The final prince, Souvanna Phouma, elected to follow a more conciliatory role mid-way between the two extremes. Of particular significance is the fact that all of the major factions of postwar Laos reflected in their leadership the continuing potency of the divine kingship tradition, graphically represented in the white umbrella and elephant symbols appearing on the new Laotian national flag. Another viewpoint shared by the rival princely leaders of Laos was their respect for the cultural and intellectual standards of France, where all of them had enjoyed schooling opportunities and privileges of residence.

One of the unfortunate effects of United States intervention in Laos after 1954 was to accentuate princely rivalry and to hasten the demoralization of the ruling anti-Communist clique at Vientiane. This was caused in part by excessive U.S. financial contributions to a misguided army-building program. In the absence of any articulate nationalist sentiment which could be mobilized to develop cohesion within the artificial Laos state, the aggravation of internal political schism by American support of Rightist Prince Boun Oum helped push the potentially reformist Pathet Lao element into full alliance with the Communist Viet Minh. Tribal friction in the mountains, tensions between hill folk and valley Lao, pro-Thai and anti-Thai feelings, and the personal rivalry and veniality of persons in high position, all operated to becloud and confuse what the United States attempted to oversimplify as a case of national freedom versus Communist aggression.

Thailand

Postwar Thailand presented an entirely different situation from that of its Buddhist neighbors to the east and north. Thailand's wartime government of Marshal Pibun, although acting under a measure of duress, collaborated with the Japanese in the prosecution of the war against both Burma and Malaya. Food and other supplies were made available to the invaders together with free access to all transportation facilities. While virtually at war with France before the start of the Far Eastern war, Thailand went further and declared war on both Britain and the United States. The country suffered, as did others, from the spiralling of prices resulting from currency inflation unmatched by consumer imports, and from manifold opportunities for personal aggrandizement on the part of corrupt officials of the government. No substantial material damages were sustained, however.

The anti-Japanese Free Thai movement headed by Pibun's political rival, Pridi, gained the ascendency at Bangkok covertly in the summer of 1944. The ostensible reason for the shift of control was rejection of Pibun's proposal to establish a new capital in the interior, possibly as a center from which to defend the nation during the expected eventual Japanese retreat. Pridi enjoyed the cooperation of the Thai ambassador to Washington, Prince Seni Promoj, who had refused to deliver Pibun's declaration of war on the U.S. and who had then aided in the formulation of Thailand's plans to assist the Allied cause. With Pridi in control, intelligence connections were established between the Allied headquarters at Kandy in Ceylon, and American agents were smuggled into the interned-alien camps of Bangkok itself. The United States elected to disregard Pibun's declaration of war, and undertook at the end of the conflict to soften the punitive aspects of the treaty terms imposed by Britain. Thus began Thailand's pro-American orientation, which was finally formalized in the SEATO alliance.

The carryover of anti-French sentiment within Thai ruling circles was reflected in the protection afforded at Bangkok to both the Lao Issara exiles in 1945-46, and in the temporary asylum accorded to King Norodom Sihanouk of Cambodia in connection with his successful efforts to exact from Paris a pledge of independence for his country. The heritage of self-seeking and corruption in high places, so greatly aggravated by Thailand's wartime experience, persisted into the postwar period with reference to American aid, and periodic somersaults of rival army factions at Bangkok continued to be an established characteristic of political life. Thus Pibun regained power in 1947, was obliged to share it after 1954, and his group finally lost out completely in 1957. The dictatorial Marshal Sarit cancelled the entire constitutional structure in the following year, and initiated an ambitious program of economic development. Some gains were impressive, but so were Sarit's defalcations. He amassed a fortune estimated at well over one hundred million dollars by the time of his death in 1963.

Whether his successor, General Thanom Kittikachorn, will be able to revive the constitutional structure as promised on the proposed basis of limited monarchy seems uncertain as of 1966. Army leadership probably will not consider it advisable to permit full expression of popular discontent over the abuse of power by the military as long as an international threat persists from both Laos and Vietnam. The situation has yet to become critical, however, for internal disaffection is not a serious problem except for increasing Communist-fomented unrest in the neglected Korat plateau in the northeast. The Bangkok government still commands the allegiance of the population generally. The symbols of divine kingship (palace, white umbrella, and sacred sword) are still potently in evidence;

the bureaucracy is intact, and the traditional Buddhist cultural milieu still holds the social order together. There are no disaffected indigenous minority groups, and the country is relatively prosperous and progressing economically.

Burma

The situation which faced postwar Burma was very discouraging. The country had suffered not only from devastating material damage during the war, but also from the long-time uprooting of its political and cultural moorings as well. Prewar political leadership under the dyarchy regime and the Constitution of 1935 was displaced by meagerly trained and inexperienced young men drawn from the ranks of the Thakin nationalists and other participants in the anti-Japanese rebellion of the Anti-Fascist Peoples Freedom League. The experienced members of the old colonial civil service, who had never been politically active, now found their official authority undermined locally by representatives of the dominant AFPFL party, who held the emasculated bureaucracy in open contempt. Already faltering governmental functions of tax collection, policing, and the dispensing of justice collapsed entirely under conditions of rebellion and violence prevailing from mid-1948 into 1951. After a modicum of order had been restored, Burma's ill-understood experiment with representative government ran afoul of domestic feuding based on personal, ethnic, and ideological rivalries. A trend toward political polarization developed in time between the anti-Western traditionalists led by fanatical younger monks and the politically-influential Westernized Thakin minority advocating the establishing of a welfare state on Marxist lines.

Premier Nu undertook the well nigh impossible task of bridging across the rifts in the body politic by his combined advocacy of democracy, a Socialist welfare state, and deepening personal and public dedication to traditionalist religious revival. His moral exhortations, however, were a poor substitute for vigorous administration. Thus the ambitious government-sponsored plans for industrial development, which would have been difficult to achieve under optimum circumstances, proved impossible of realization. Although Nu's personal charm and his charismatic role as a patron of religion enhanced his election appeal, an excessive religious commitment hampered efforts to curb the growing indiscipline of politically vocal monks. They took advantage of his deferential posture to intimidate both voters and elected members of the parliament and eventually threatened the religious freedom of minority groups in defiance of

Nu's wishes. Premier Nu carried through his election pledge of 1960 to make Buddhism the official state religion only by exercising political coercion, and amid threatening communal violence. The supplementary amendment designed to protect the freedom of religious minority groups was passed in September 1961, at a legislative session convened irregularly at 4:30 A.M. in order to avoid violating a monk's picket line scheduled for 5:30 A.M. Nu qualified as a ruler-patron of Buddhism, but as a mere *elected* official he lacked both kingly status and governing authority.

General Ne Win's military coup of March 1962, was designed ostensibly to arrest the threatened disintegration of the Burma Union both territorially and politically. But his repudiation of democracy and his authoritarian sponsorship of the "Burmese Road to Socialism" attracted no civilian following and came to rest on naked military force. The costs to Burma by 1966 in terms of economic paralysis and denial of individual opportunity to speak and act freely were staggeringly high. Burma's historical experiences since the 1920's were taking a heavy toll.

Buddhist Southeast Asia as a whole, as of 1966, is a community of states in transition. They face unresolved problems of adjustment, not only internally and with reference to immediate neighbors, but also with respect to world developments over which the peoples of the region itself have little control. The peoples merit genuine understanding and patient assistance from the outside as they struggle with manifold difficulties.

The reading materials available for general Southeast Asian history and for Theravada Buddhist lands in particular are highly disparate in both number and quality. The able French scholar Georges Coedès opened up the field generally with his *Les États Hindouisés d'Indochine et d'Indonésie* (Paris, 1948), an account limited to the pre-European period. A more recent study by Coedès entitled *Peuples de la Peninsule Indochinoise: Histoire—Civilisation* (Paris, 1962) carried his account into modern times. Two similar works in English concerned mainly with artistic aspects of Indian cultural contributions were H. G. Quaritch Wales, *The Making of Greater India* (London, 1951) and Reginald Le May, *The Culture of South-East Asia: the Heritage of India* (London, 1954). The first general historical survey in English was Brian Harrison's *South-East Asia: A Short History* (New York, 1954), which was followed in 1955 by D. G. E. Hall's detailed political narrative entitled *A History of Southeast Asia*. Hall's revised edition of 1964 included an additional chapter on the Philippines and one on "Independence" since 1950. A companion history less concerned with political minutiae and relating to a broader historical and cultural context was John F. Cady's *Southeast Asia: Its Historical Development* (New York, 1964), which carried the narrative to the end of World War II. Two particularly useful monographs touching different aspects of the Southeast Asian situation were Kenneth P. Landon's *South-East Asia, Crossroads of Religion* (Chicago, 1947) and Virginia Thompson's *Minority Problems in Southeast Asia* (Stanford, 1955). Russell H. Fifield provided a highly competent and objective survey of *The Diplomacy of Southeast Asia* (New York, 1958), and George McTurnan Kahin edited successive revisions of his standard *Governments and Politics in Southeast Asia* (Ithaca, 1959 and 1963).

With respect to Burma, there is available no adequate account of the history of the country in its entirety. G. E. Harvey's first *History of Burma* (London, 1925) covered the story down to the advent of British control in 1824, which was followed by his *British Rule in Burma, 1824-1942* (London, 1946). Both were inadequate. John Nisbet's *Burmah Under British Rule* (2 vols.; London, 1901) and Arthur P. Phayre's *His-*

143

tory of Burma (London, 1883) were also limited in their perspectives. A satisfactory brief summary, although focussed mainly on the European period, is D. G. E. Hall's *Burma* (London, 1956) in the Hutchinson "University Library Series." Hall also edited *Michael Symes: Journal of his Second Embassy to the Court of Ava in 1802* (London, 1955) and contributed to it an excellent introductory characterization of Burma's government at the time of Symes's visit. The standard account of Burma's history since 1784 by John F. Cady, entitled *A History of Modern Burma* (Ithaca, 1958 and 1960), centered mainly on the influence exerted by British India, the impact of colonial rule, and the twentieth-century revival of Burmese nationalism. The best account of Burma since its achievement of independence in 1948 was Hugh Tinker's *The Union of Burma* (Oxford, 1957 and 1959). Lucian W. Pye's *Politics, Personality, and Nation Building: Burma's Search for Identity* (London and New Haven, 1962) applied techniques of social scientists, but lacked historical depth. The best description of Burma's prewar economy is J. R. Andrus' *Burmese Economic Life* (Stanford, 1947).

A number of British Civil Servants contributed useful monographs based on their Burma experiences. The best include Henry Yule, *A Narrative of the Mission . . . to the Court of Ava in 1855* (London, 1858), James George Scott (Shway Yoe), *The Burman: His Life and Notions* (London, 1882, 1896, 1910, and New York, 1963), Herbert Thirkell White, *A Civil Servant in Burma* (London, 1913), and various works by John S. Furnivall, especially his *Progress and Welfare in Southeast Asia* (New York, 1941) and *Colonial Policy and Practice* (New York, 1948 and 1956). Furnivall was particularly sensitive to the problems connected with the functioning of plural societies under colonial rule. F. S. V. Donnison's *Public Administration in Burma* (London, 1953) traced the evolution of colonial rule. Maurice Collis, a British judge, contributed a classic interpretation of rising national tensions in his *Trials in Burma* (London, 1945). Creditable works by Burman authors have been relatively few. The best include Mi Mi Khaing's *The Burmese Family* (Bombay, 1946), Maung Maung's *Burma in the Family of Nations* (Amsterdam, 1956), Thakin Nu's *Burma Under the Japanese, Pictures and Portraits* (New York, 1954), and U Ba U's *My Burma; the Autobiography of a President* (New York, 1959). The preliminary draft of the Human Relations Area Files survey of Burma, edited by Frank N. Trager, has not been published in an edited edition. Donald Eugene Smith contributed a perceptive study of *Religion and Politics in Burma* (Princeton, 1965).

The standard history of Siam is W. A. R. Wood's *A History of Siam to A. D. 1781, with Supplement* (London, 1926 and Bangkok, 1933). Walter Vella contributed substantially to the modern period by his *Siam Under Rama III* (New York, 1957) and his significant *The Impact of the West on the Government of Siam* (Berkeley, 1955). James C. Ingram's *Economic Change in Thailand Since 1850* (Stanford, 1955) explained factors contributing to the tardiness of Siam's economic development. Court life at Bangkok was described by Prince Chula Chakrabonse's *Lords of Life* (London, 1960), and Abbot Low Moffatt wrote a sympathetic study of *Mongkut, the King of Siam* (Ithaca, 1961). Kenneth P. Landon's *Siam in Transition* (Shanghai, 1939) and Virginia Thompson's *Thailand: the New Siam* (New York, 1941) carried the story down to World War II. The postwar political scene was described in John Coast's realistic *Some Aspects of Siamese Politics* (New York, 1953) and in David A. Wilson's more thoroughgoing *Politics in Thailand* (Ithaca, 1962). D. Insor's *Thailand, A Political, Social, and Economic Analysis* (New York, 1963) contains useful information on cultural and administrative problems.

The prewar description of Thai culture by Reginald Stuart Le May, *An Asian Arcadie; The Land and Peoples of Northern Siam* (Cambridge and New York, 1926) can be supplemented by various chapters of the highly informative monograph of the Human Relations Area Files, *Thailand: Its People, Its Society, Its Culture* (New Haven, 1958), edited by Wendell Blanchard. The Siam Society in 1958 sponsored publication of Erik Seidenfadan's *The Thai Peoples*. Two descriptions of Bangkok and environs, as of 1821-22, survive in John Crawford's *Journal of an Embassy . . . to the Court of Siam and Cochin-China* (London, 1828) and in George Finlayson's *The Mission to Siam and Hué . . . in 1821-1822* (London, 1826). Kenneth E. Wells has described *Thai Buddhism: its Rites and Activities* (Bangkok, 1939) and has also contributed a *History of Protestant Work in Thailand, 1828-1958* (Bangkok, 1958). The activities, beliefs, and social institutions of the Thai peasantry were portrayed in John E. de Young's *Village Life in Modern Thailand* (Berkeley, 1955). William Skinner's treatment of *Chinese Society in Thailand* (Ithaca, 1957) was substantially superior to Victor Purcell's more general *The Chinese in South-East Asia* (Oxford, 1951).

Most of the voluminous writings of French scholars concern the more important Vietnamese portion of French Indochina rather then Cambodia and Laos. Two general histories of Cambodia can be cited: A. Dauphin-Meunier's *Histoire du Cambodge* (Paris, 1961) and A. Leclerc's older book, *Histoire du Cambodge* (Paris, 1914) along with Martin F. Herz's *A Short History of Cambodia from the Days of Angkor to the Present* (New York, 1958). Aside from George Coedès' classic *Pour Mieux Comprendre Angkor* (Paris, 1947), the most rewarding discussions of ancient Angkor are Lawrence Palmer Briggs' *The Ancient Khmer Empire* (Philadelphia, 1951) and E. E. Smith's translation of a study by Bernard P. Groslier and Jacques Arthaud entitled *The Arts and Civilization of Angkor* (New York, 1957). The useful Hutchinson Library series volume, by A. H. Broderick, is entitled *Little Vehicle: Cambodia and Laos* (London, 1949). Groslier's excellent monograph on 16th century Cambodia is entitled *Angkor et le Cambodge au siècle XVIe d'aprés les sources portugaises et espagnoles* (Paris, 1958). It includes aerial photographic reconstructions of the ancient Angkor irrigation system. Most writings on the last century of Cambodia's history deal mainly with French imperialist policy. John F. Cady's *The Roots of French Imperialism in Eastern Asia* (Ithaca, 1954) characterized French political and cultural motivation. The basic study by Steven Henry Roberts, *History of French Colonial Policy* (2 vols.; London, 1929) concerns Cambodia and Laos only marginally. Both Virginia Thompson's *French Indo-China* (New York, 1937) and Thomas E. Ennis' *French Policy and Development in Indochina* (Chicago, 1936) center attention on Vietnam and are problem-oriented. One of the few studies focussing on the Cambodian people themselves is the Human Relations Area Files monograph edited by David J. Steinberg, *Cambodia: Its People, Its Society, Its Culture* (New Haven, 1959). Roger M. Smith's, *Cambodia's Foreign Policy* (Ithaca, 1965) covers the years since 1954.

Materials on the history of Laos are few. The old standard description was by Lucien de Reinach, *Le Leos*, (2 vols.; Paris, 1901 and 1911). A shorter descriptive study edited by René de Berval is available in English under the title, *Kingdom of Laos: The Land of the Million Elephants and the White Parasol* (Saigon, 1959). Joel Martin Halpern has prepared a number of valuable studies on postwar Laos, the most substantial being *Aspects of Village Life and Culture Change in Laos* (New York, 1958), which was prepared for the Council on Economic and Cultural Affairs. The Human Relations Area Files study edited by Frank M. Le Bar and Adrienne Suddard, *Laos* (New Haven, 1959), contains useful chapters on geography, population, languages, and social structure, but it is deficient as history and suffers for having been forced into a prefabricated mold. The best account of American involvement in Laos after 1954 is A. J. Dommen's *Conflict in Laos* (New York, 1965).

A great deal of valuable historical material relating to Burma and Siam can be found in the files of the *Journal of the Burma Research Society*, especially the contributions of G. C. Luce, and in the *Journal of the Siam Society*. Particularly promising is the relatively new *Journal of Southeast Asian History*, published in Malaysia, and also the *Asian Studies*, recently sponsored by the University of the Philippines. The leading American journals dealing with the region are *The Journal of Asian Studies*, the *Asian Survey*, and the Institute of Pacific Relations' *Pacific Affairs*.

INDEX